Improving Access to Economic Opportunity: Nonmetropolitan Labor Markets in An Urban Society

Improving Access to Economic Opportunity:

Nonmetropolitan Labor Markets in An Urban Society

Niles M. Hansen
Center for Economic Development
University of Texas

Ballinger Publishing Company ● **Cambridge, Mass.**
A Subsidiary of J.B. Lippincott Company

Copyright © 1976 by Ballinger Publishing Company.

Reproduction in whole or in part permitted for any purpose of the United States Government.

International Standard Book Number: 0-88410-289-0

Library of Congress Catalog Card Number: 75-38800

Printed in the United States of America

Library of Congress Cataloging in Publication Data

Hansen, Niles M
    Improving access to economic opportunity.

    Bibliography: p.
    Includes index.
    1. Labor supply—United States. 2. Manpower policy—United States. 3. Regional planning—United States. 4. Community—United States.
I. Title.
HD5724.H283   331.1'1'0973   75-38800
ISBN 0-88410-289-0

Contents

List of Figures

List of Maps

ix

List of Tables

Preface

Despite the fact that any factor that has a significant effect on the location of population and economic activity will also have important implications for manpower policy, federal economic development and manpower policies have seldom been coordinated. The present study critically examines the nature and consequences of these policies for nonmetropolitan areas, and suggests how they might be better integrated within the framework of the substate planning and development districts that have been formed in all the states in recent years.

The first two chapters describe the nature of the American urban system and its relationship to nonmetropolitan areas, and examine problems faced by the latter in what is essentially an urban society. Chapter three discusses efforts to bring jobs to nonmetropolitan areas by means of regional development policies. The growth center strategy is evaluated in both theoretical and empirical terms. Because problems of creating greater access to economic opportunity are closely bound up with the spatial organization of labor markets, the rationales behind various delineations of functional economic areas are analyzed in Chapter four. Chapter five assesses the roles of substate regional planning and the A–95 review process in coordinating federal, state and local policies and programs in nonmetropolitan areas. Chapter six discusses the implications of the Comprehensive Employment and Training Act of 1973 for nonmetropolitan manpower planning and examines in detail the unusual efforts that have been made in Tennessee to integrate CETA programs with area development efforts in a substate planning district context. Journey to work problems in nonmetropolitan areas are dealt with in Chapters seven and eight. Chapter seven also analyzes differences in commuting patterns and welfare indicators among (1) nonmetropolitan regions which represent potentially viable functional labor market areas, (2) relatively nearby metropolitan areas and (3) dispersed urban regions. Recent innovations in rural transportation are investigated in Chapter eight; special attention is given to a novel program being instituted in South Carolina with CETA funds. The final chapter summarizes the findings of the previous chapters and suggests approaches for improving access to economic opportunity in nonmetropolitan areas.

Chapter three is a revised version of "An Evaluation of Growth Center Theory and Practice," a paper originally presented at the Conference on National Settlement Systems and Strategies, International Institute for Applied Systems Analysis, Laxenburg, Austria, December 16-19, 1974. The original paper, along with some other papers presented at the conference, will appear in 1976 in a special number of *Environment and Planning*. Chapter four is a revised version of a research report prepared for the International Institute for Applied Systems Analysis. This report, "A Critique of Economic Regionalizations for the United States" (RR-75-32) was published by the Institute in 1975.

The author is indebted to numerous persons for their assistance in preparing this volume. The scores of government officials—federal, state and local—and academic colleagues consulted preclude individual identification, although it would not have been possible to carry out the study without their generous cooperation. I would, however, like to acknowledge the especially important contributions of Rita Ellison, Pamela Pape, James Peach, Carol Pfrommer, and Koren Sherrill, colleagues in the Center for Economic Development, University of Texas.

Finally, these combined efforts would not have been possible without the support of the Office of Research and Development, Manpower Administration, U.S. Department of Labor. In this regard I am particularly indebted to Howard Rosen, Anna-Stina Ericson, Ellen Schgal, Herman Travis and Etta Williamson.

Niles M. Hansen

November 1975

Chapter One

Introduction

OBJECTIVE OF THE STUDY

This study is primarily concerned with the spatial organization of nonmetropolitan labor markets, and in particular with feasible means for giving workers and potential workers in nonmetropolitan areas greater access to manpower services and to more and better employment opportunities. The emphasis is on problems related to the frictions associated with distance, although it also is recognized that this access often is limited by social and political factors such as racial discrimination and sheer neglect in such areas as information diffusion and human resource development.

PLACE OF RESIDENCE AND ECONOMIC STATUS

Census Definitions

Given the great variety of population settlement and density patterns that prevail in this country—to say nothing of attitudes and life styles—it is somewhat arbitrary to draw fine rural-urban and metropolitan-nonmetropolitan distinctions. U.S. Bureau of the Census practice includes in the rural population all persons living in the open country or in towns with fewer than 2500 inhabitants. The urban population includes all persons living in urbanized areas or, outside of urbanized areas, in places with 2500 or more people. An urbanized area—a concept adopted by the bureau in 1950—contains at least one city of 50,000 or more population (or twin central cities with a combined population of at least 50,000) and is divided into a central city (or cities) and the remainder of the contiguous, closely settled area. However, it is now more conventional to differentiate metropolitan and nonmetropolitan residence categories in terms of Standard Metropolitan Statistical Areas. There are a number of criteria for defining an SMSA but essentially it must have one city of at least 50,000 inhabitants and it includes the county of the central city and those adjacent counties which are determined to be metropolitan in character and economically and socially integrated with the county of the central city. Tables 1–1 and 1–2 present data for the United States using these definitions.

Poverty Incidence

Table 1–3 shows persons and families in low income status in 1973. Low income status in effect indicates poverty status. The former term replaced the latter during the Nixon administration, but the methods for determining the relevant numbers of persons and families have remained the same. For the sake of brevity I shall refer to poverty as poverty. In 1973, 11.1 percent of all Americans lived under poverty conditions; 8.8 percent of all families were in poverty status. The corresponding values for nonfarm residents were 11.0 percent and 8.6 percent, respectively, and for farm families 13.4 percent and 11.6 percent. Although a great deal of attention has properly been given to the plight of the central city poor, the proportion of poor people in nonmetropolitan areas is just as great as that in central cities, 14.0 percent. The proportion of nonmetropolitan families in poverty (11.2 percent) is even greater than that in central cities (10.9 percent). The term "low income areas" refers to census tracts or minor civil divisions (townships, districts, etc.) in which 20 percent or more of the population is below the poverty threshold level. For all persons and for families, the proportion of low income area residents who are poor is less in nonmetropolitan areas than in either central cities or suburbs of SMSAs. The fact that rural poverty tends to be more geographically diffuse no doubt accounts in part for the relative neglect of the rural poor. For all types of residence shown in Table 1–3, the proportion of blacks in poverty is considerably greater than that of whites. The incidence of poverty among blacks in nonmetropolitan areas is much greater than that among metropolitan blacks, even those in central cities. Although these data refer to areas defined by the Bureau of the Census, the importance of access to metropolitan opportunities is evident even when other spatial concepts are used.

URBAN FIELDS

A persuasive case can be made for spatial concepts which are more general than those already discussed, primarily on the ground that it is increasingly difficult to distinguish what is urban from what is rural. For example, residential location preference surveys indicate that most Americans prefer to live in small towns or rural areas, but within easy commuting distance of metropolitan amenities.[1] In keeping with this phenomenon, John Friedmann and John Miller foresee

Table 1–1. United States Population in Urban Places, Urbanized Areas and Rural Areas by Race, 1950 to 1970 (in thousands, except percent)

Year and Area	Total	White	Negro and Other	*Percent Distribution*		
				Total	White	Negro and Other
1950, total population	151,326	135,150	16,176	100.0	100.0	100.0
Urban	96,847	86,864	9,983	64.0	64.3	61.7
Inside urbanized areas	69,249	61,925	7,324	45.8	45.8	45.3
Central cities	48,377	42,042	6,335	32.0	31.1	39.2
Urban fringe	20,872	19,883	989	13.8	14.7	6.1
Outside urbanized areas	27,598	24,939	2,659	18.2	18.5	16.4
Rural	54,479	48,286	6,193	36.0	35.7	38.3
1960, total population	179,323	158,832	20,491	100.0	100.0	100.0
Urban	125,269	110,428	14,840	69.9	69.5	72.4
Inside urbanized areas	95,848	83,770	12,079	53.5	52.7	58.9
Central cities	57,975	47,627	10,348	32.3	30.0	50.5
Urban fringe	37,873	36,143	1,731	21.1	22.8	8.4
Outside urbanized areas	29,420	26,658	2,762	16.4	16.8	13.5
Rural	54,054	48,403	5,651	30.1	30.5	27.6
1970, total population	203,212	177,749	25,463	100.0	100.0	100.0
Urban	149,325	128,773	20,552	73.5	72.4	80.7
Inside urbanized areas	118,447	100,952	17,495	58.3	56.8	68.7
Central cities	63,922	49,547	14,375	31.5	27.9	56.5
Urban fringe	54,525	51,405	3,120	26.8	28.9	12.3
Outside urbanized areas	30,878	27,822	3,057	15.2	15.7	12.0
Rural	53,887	48,976	4,911	26.5	27.6	19.3

Source: U.S. Bureau of the Census, *Statistical Abstract of the United States, 1972* (Washington, D.C.: Government Printing Office, 1972), p. 16.

Table 1-2. United States Population in Standard Metropolitan Statistical Areas and Nonmetropolitan Areas by Race, 1950 to 1970 (in thousands, except percent)

Residence and Race	Population			1970		Percent Change		Average Annual Change	
	1950	1960	Total	Percent		1950–1960	1960–1970	1950–1960	1960–1970
TOTAL	151,326	179,323	203,212	100.0		18.5	13.3	1.7	1.3
Standard metropolitan statistical areas	94,579	119,595	139,419	68.6		26.4	16.6	2.3	1.5
Central cities	53,696	59,947	63,797	31.4		11.6	6.4	1.1	0.6
Outside central cities	40,883	59,648	75,622	37.2		45.9	26.8	3.8	2.4
Nonmetropolitan areas	56,747	59,728	63,793	31.4		5.3	6.8	0.5	0.7
WHITE	135,150	158,832	177,749	100.0		17.5	11.9	1.6	1.1
Standard metropolitan statistical areas	85,099	105,180	120,579	67.8		23.6	14.6	2.1	1.4
Central cities	46,791	49,440	49,430	27.8		5.7	-0.2	0.6	-0.1
Outside central cities	38,308	55,741	71,148	40.0		45.5	27.6	3.8	2.5
Nonmetropolitan areas	50,051	53,652	57,170	32.2		7.2	6.6	0.7	0.6
NEGRO	14,972	18,792	22,580	100.0		25.5	20.2	2.3	1.9
Standard metropolitan statistical areas	8,850	12,710	16,771	74.3		43.6	32.0	3.6	2.8
Central cities	6,608	9,950	13,140	58.2		50.6	32.1	4.1	2.8
Outside central cities	2,242	2,760	3,630	16.1		23.1	31.5	2.1	2.8
Nonmetropolitan areas	6,122	6,083	5,810	25.7		-0.6	-4.5	-0.1	-0.5

Source: U.S. Bureau of the Census, *Statistical Abstract of the United States, 1972* (Washington, D.C.: Government Printing Office, 1972), p. 16.

Table 1-3. Persons and Families in Low Income Status in 1973, Type of Residence and Race of Head
(Numbers in thousands. Persons and families as of March 1974)

		All Races	
		Below Low Income Level	
Type of Residence	*Total*	*Number*	*Percent of Total*
PERSONS			
United States	207,621	22,973	11.1
Nonfarm	198,075	21,689	11.0
Farm	9,546	1,283	13.4
Metropolitan areas[1]	141,795	13,759	9.7
Inside central cities	61,526	8,594	14.0
In low income areas	13,450	4,363	32.4
Outside central cities	80,269	5,165	6.4
In low income areas	4,486	1,029	22.9
Nonmetropolitan areas[1]	65,826	9,214	14.0
In low income areas	23,473	5,257	22.4
North and West	142,008	12,912	9.1
South	65,613	10,061	15.3
FAMILIES			
United States	55,053	4,828	8.8
Nonfarm	52,511	4,533	8.6
Farm	2,542	295	11.6
Metropolitan areas[1]	37,317	2,838	7.6
Inside central cities	16,019	1,753	10.9
In low income areas	3,157	902	28.6
Outside central cities	21,297	1,086	5.1
In low income areas	1,136	218	19.2
Nonmetropolitan areas[1]	17,736	1,990	11.2
In low income areas	6,289	1,125	17.9
North and West	37,410	2,685	7.2
South	17,643	2,143	12.1

table continued on pages 6 & 7

Table 1–3. Continued

Type of Residence	Total	White Below Low Income Level Number	White Below Low Income Level Percent of Total
PERSONS			
United States	181,185	15,142	8.4
Nonfarm	172,327	14,159	8.2
Farm	8,858	983	11.1
Metropolitan areas[1]	121,638	8,452	6.9
Inside central cities	46,392	4,305	9.3
In low income areas	5,535	1,303	23.5
Outside central cities	75,246	4,147	5.5
In low income areas	3,224	670	20.8
Nonmetropolitan areas[1]	59,547	6,690	11.2
In low income areas	19,181	3,286	17.1
North and West	128,511	9,741	7.6
South	52,674	5,401	10.3
FAMILIES			
United States	48,919	3,219	6.6
Nonfarm	46,523	2,984	6.4
Farm	2,397	235	9.8
Metropolitan areas[1]	32,584	1,723	5.3
Inside central cities	12,463	851	6.8
In low income areas	1,337	256	19.2
Outside central cities	20,121	872	4.3
In low income areas	830	141	17.0
Nonmetropolitan areas[1]	16,335	1,496	9.2
In low income areas	5,357	747	14.0
North and West	34,242	2,015	5.9
South	14,677	1,204	8.2

Table 1–3. Continued

Type of Residence	Total	Black Below Low Income Level Number	Percent of Total
PERSONS			
United States	23,512	7,388	31.4
Nonfarm	22,852	7,102	31.1
Farm	659	287	43.5
Metropolitan areas[1]	17,700	4,998	28.2
Inside central cities	13,701	4,062	29.6
In low income areas	7,695	2,998	39.0
Outside central cities	3,999	936	23.4
In low income areas	1,209	357	29.6
Nonmetropolitan areas[1]	5,811	2,390	41.1
In low income areas	4,159	1,903	45.7
North and West	11,086	2,877	25.9
South	12,425	4,511	36.3
FAMILIES			
United States	5,440	1,527	28.1
Nonfarm	5,304	1,471	27.7
Farm	136	56	40.8
Metropolitan areas[1]	4,154	1,057	25.4
Inside central cities	3,223	860	26.7
In low income areas	1,772	636	35.9
Outside central cities	931	197	21.1
In low income areas	292	77	26.4
Nonmetropolitan areas[1]	1,286	470	36.5
In low income areas	905	368	40.6
North and West	2,596	614	23.6
South	2,844	913	32.1

1. Based on SMSAs as defined in the 1970 census.
Source: U.S. Bureau of the Census, *Current Population Reports,* series P-60, no. 94, "Characteristics of the Low-Income Population" (Washington, D.C.: Government Printing Office, July 1974), p. 10.

a new scale of urban living that will extend far beyond existing metropolitan cores and penetrate deeply into the periphery. Relations of dominance and dependency will be transcended. The older established centers, together with the intermetropolitan peripheries that envelop them, will constitute the new ecological unit of American's post-industrial society that will replace traditional concepts of the city and metropolis. This basic element of the emerging spatial order we shall call the *urban field*.

The urban field may be viewed as an enlargement of the space for urban living that extends far beyond the boundaries of existing metropolitan areas—defined primarily in terms of commuting to a central city of "metropolitan" size—into the open landscape of the periphery. This change to a larger scale of urban life is already underway, encouraged by changes in technology, economics, and preferred social behavior. Eventually the urban field may even come to be acknowledged as a community of *shared* interests, although these interests may be more strongly oriented to specific functions than to area. They will be shared because to a large extent they will overlap and complement each other within a specific locational matrix. Because urban fields will be large, with populations of upwards of one million, their social and cultural life will form a rich and varied pattern capable of satisfying most human aspirations within a local setting.[2]

For the time being, however, Friedmann and Miller acknowledge that

Except for thinly populated parts of the American interior, the intermetropolitan periphery includes all areas that intervene among metropolitan regions that are, as it were, the reverse image of the trend towards large scale concentrated settlement that has persisted in this country for over half a century. Like a devil's mirror, much of it has developed a socio-economic profile that perversely reflects the very opposite of metropolitan virility.[3]

LABOR MARKET PARTICIPATION IN DAILY URBAN SYSTEMS

In a similar vein, Brian Berry has challenged the use of SMSAs as basic units of urban analysis on the ground that people no longer live and work in the same place, and that separation of residence and work place continues to increase. Berry's alternative unit of spatial accounting is the Daily Urban System, which is discussed in some detail in Chapter Four. However, it should be pointed out here that Berry's analysis of the commuting behavior of the American population in 1960, which provided the basis for his delineation of a nationally exhaustive set of Daily Urban Systems, clearly indicated that lack of access to metropolitan areas was detrimental to well-being.

Berry found that all but 5 percent of the country's population lives within the daily commuting field of metropolitan centers. (As will be noted later in this chapter, the 5 percent value is misleading. Nevertheless, the distance–decay of welfare discussed in the rest of the paragraph retains its relevance.) These fields spread over the entire country except where population densities are less than two persons per square mile or where there are national parks and Indian reservations. Degree of metropolitan labor market participation was found to be the key variable in the "regional welfare syndrome," an index of the pattern of urban influence on the surrounding hinterlands' level of economic well-being as measured by such factors as income and employment. In general, degree of labor market participation (daily commuting to employment in the central city) declines with increasing distance from the city, as do the average values of farm land and buildings, median family income, median school years completed, rate of population increase (which is negative in the peripheries), and population gain through migration (which also becomes negative in the more outlying areas). Proportion of families with annual incomes less than $3000 and the unemployment rate are both directly related to distance from the central city. Thus, the lowest levels of welfare are at the edges of metropolitan fields and especially in the nonurban interstices between them. When closely spaced metropolitan centers have overlapping labor markets, so that the population of one center can take advantage of employment opportunities in another, the decline in welfare levels with distance from the centers is reduced or eliminated. In contrast, the wider the centers are spread, the lower are the levels to which regional welfare measures fall. Berry found that, in general, "labor markets appear to need to be of greater than 250,000 population to be viable parts of the urban system"[4] and that "very few cities of less than 50,000 population appear to have any impact on the regional welfare syndrone."[5]

NONCOMMUTER COUNTIES

Definition
Because commuting patterns play such a large role in the delineation of functional economic areas, it is instructive to consider more closely the nature of rural areas with noncommuting populations. A recent study[6] prepared by the Economic Research Service, U.S. Department of Agriculture, finds that over half of the nation's counties are far removed from the economic, social and cultural benefits usually available in larger cities (see Map 1–1). Three categories of counties are identified in this analysis. *Urban counties* are defined to be counties with 25,000 or more urban population, or having 10,000 or more nonfarm wage and salary jobs in 1970. Counties from which 10 percent or more of all workers commuted to jobs located in

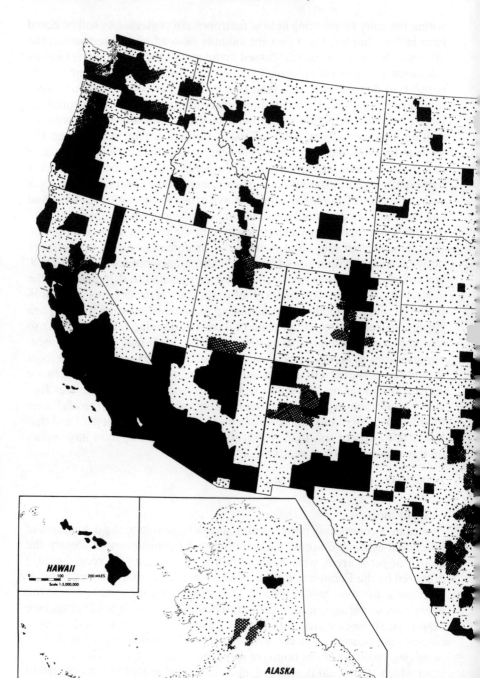

Map 1–1. Urban/Employment Centers, Commuter Counties and Rural/Small Town Noncommuter Counties.

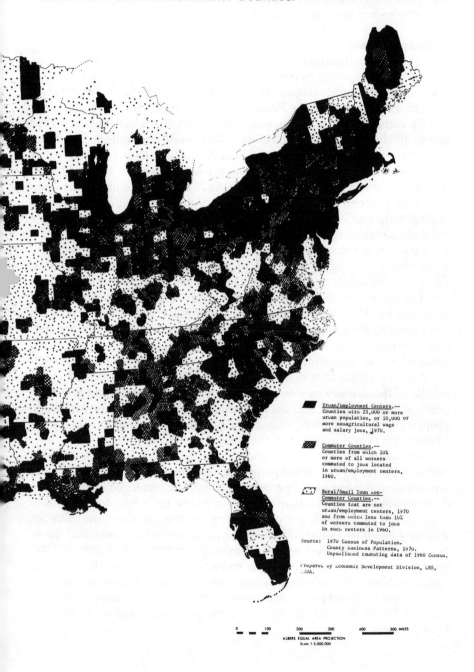

Urban/Employment Centers.--
Counties with 25,000 or more
urban population, or 10,000 or
more nonagricultural wage
and salary jobs, 1970.

Commuter Counties.--
Counties from which 10%
or more of all workers
commuted to jobs located
in urban/employment centers,
1960.

Rural/Small Town Non-
Commuter Counties.--
Counties that are not
urban/employment centers, 1970
and from which less than 10%
of workers commuted to jobs
in such centers in 1960.

Source: 1970 Census of Population.
County Business Patterns, 1970.
Unpublished commuting data of 1960 Census.

Prepared by Economic Development Division, ERS,
USDA.

0   100   200   300   400   500 MILES

ALBERS EQUAL AREA PROJECTION
Scale 1:5,000,000

urban counties (as defined in 1960, the most recent date for which commuting data were available) are defined to be *commuter counties*. The remaining counties are the *noncommuter counties*.

Characteristics

It may be noted that the expansion of the Interstate Highway System, as well as other highway systems, during the 1960s certainly induced increased commuting in relation to the patterns that prevailed in 1960. The 10 percent standard used in the Economic Research Service study was deliberately conservative to compensate for expected changes between 1960 and 1970. Nevertheless, on this basis, 1718 counties had little or no linkage with urban centers; their population in 1970 was 24 million, or 12 percent of the national total. The noncommuting population obviously would have been even greater if commuting to SMSAs had been examined rather than commuting to counties with 25,000 or more urban population. (Berry's finding, cited earlier, that 5 percent of the nation's population lived within the daily commuting fields of SMSAs in 1960 seems strained. Even if this were true on the basis of, say, a 5 percent commuting field, it would still mean that 19 out of 20 workers did not commute. Calvin Beale of the Economic Research Service, U.S. Department of Agriculture, has indicated to me in conversation that in 1960 about 40 million nonmetropolitan residents lived in counties where less than 5 percent of the population commuted to SMSAs. This amounted to two-thirds of the entire nonmetropolitan population. On this basis it would appear that Berry classified as a commuter county any county from which anyone commuted to an SMSA!)

Map 1–1 shows that noncommuter counties are concentrated in the middle of the country as well as in many parts of the West and South. In contrast, the Northeast and the industrial Middle West account for a large proportion of both the 806 urban counties and the 572 commuter counties. Commuting also is common in the South Atlantic states.

The noncommuter counties tend to have small populations. Moreover, between 1960 and 1970 they experienced net outmigration of 10 percent and a population decline of 1.2 percent. In 1960, the incidence of poverty in noncommuter counties—four persons in every ten—was double that in urban counties. In 1967, per capita income in the noncommuter counties was only about two-thirds of that in the combined urban-commuter counties (see Table 1–4). Although the national incidence of poverty has declined since then, the evidence suggests that the rural-urban differential has remained about the same in absolute terms. Similarly, while the noncommuter counties have 12 percent of the nation's occupied housing units, they account for 21 percent of the total number of crowded or inadequate housing units.[7]

Table 1–4.   Per capita Income by Urban Commuter and Noncommuter County Groups, 1959 and 1967

Geographic Divisions	Urban and Commuter Counties		Annual Change		Noncommuter Counties		Annual Change	
	1959	1967	Amount	Percent	1959	1967	Amount	Percent
New England	$2,323	$3,412	$136	4.9	$1,576	$2,456	$110	5.7
Middle Atlantic	2,495	3,617	140	4.8	1,659	2,532	109	5.4
East North Central	2,370	3,488	135	4.8	1,517	2,395	110	5.8
West North Central	2,265	3,289	128	4.8	1,499	2,436	117	6.2
South Atlantic	1,870	2,857	123	5.4	1,134	1,919	98	6.8
East South Central	1,642	2,460	102	5.2	965	1,672	98	7.1
West South Central	1,874	2,758	110	4.9	1,432	2,172	92	5.3
Mountain	2,100	2,843	93	3.9	1,752	2,525	97	4.7
Pacific	2,547	3,598	129	4.4	2,122	2,941	102	4.2
United States	2,250	3,278	128	4.8	1,399	2,219	102	5.9

Gap from U.S. Average Per Capita Level of Income[1]

Geographic Divisions	Urban and Commuter Counties		Noncommuter Counties	
	1959	1967	1959	1967
New England	$ 8	$ 262	–$739	–$694
Middle Atlantic	180	467	–656	–618
East North Central	55	298	–798	–755
West North Central	50	139	–816	–714
South Atlantic	–444	–293	–1,181	–1,231
East South Central	–673	–690	–1,350	–1,478
West South Central	–441	–392	–883	–978
Mountain	–215	–307	–563	–626
Pacific	232	448	–193	–209
United States	115	128	–736	–931

Source: U.S. Department of Agriculture, Economic Research Service, *Characteristics of U.S. Rural Areas With Noncommuting Population*, prepared for the Senate Committee on Agriculture and Forestry, 92 Cong., 2d sess. (Washington, D.C.: Government Printing Office, 1972), p. 23.

1. Gap calculated from U.S. average per capita incomes of $2,135 in 1959 and $3,150 in 1967.

SPECIAL PROBLEMS OF
RURAL RESIDENTS

Although the degree to which a town or county is ''rural'' may be disputed, rural areas and their residents often have special problems and characteristics related in varying degree to their relatively low income status and to population loss, which tends to drain off the younger and more able members of the community. The unemployment rate in rural areas is underestimated because many rural jobs are not covered under unemployment insurance; moreover, it does not take into account the low labor force participation by some groups. Many rural areas lack most of the elements of functioning governments as well as a wide range of public and private services taken for granted in cities. The local revenue base tends to be inadequate to provide needed public services and there is very little future prospect of improvement from local sources. Nonfarm employment opportunities, to the extent that they exist, may be limited to marginal low wage industries. Rural areas have relatively high proportions of both persons under 21 and older people; many new entrants to the labor market have no work experience and the private employment prospects of the older workers are dim. Education levels in rural areas tend to be relatively low both in terms of years of schooling and of the quality of the educational experience. Many older persons, and particularly nonwhites, are functional illiterates, although this phenomenon is not confined to this group.[8] Thus, as Dale Hathaway points out,

> in rural areas you are not dealing with a labor force that is temporarily unemployed because of cyclical shifts but with a population that has been and will be chronically unemployed or underemployed. You are not dealing with governments with a full array of public service functions but with governments that offer limited public services. You are not dealing with governments that are fully and adequately staffed by full-time professionals but with governments that exist more on paper than in reality.[9]

LACK OF HUMAN RESOURCE AND
MANPOWER PROGRAMS

Despite the obvious educational, social and manpower needs of rural areas, the characteristics just discussed have frequently limited their ability to attract or effectively use federal funds. It has been estimated that the proportion of federal expenditures for vocational education and certain manpower programs going to primarily rural counties in fiscal year 1969 may have been less than half these counties' proportion of the national population. Their share of federal outlays for housing and community aids and for health services and care was also relatively low.[10]

"The typical farm operator derives most of his income from off-farm work, but there are very few manpower programs to help small farmers upgrade their farming capabilities and acquire nonfarm skills to improve off-farm earnings."[11] This situation exists in large part because manpower programs have usually been developed in response to urban problems and are not readily adaptable to rural conditions. The 1971 Manpower Report of the President acknowledged that:

> The limited employment services available in rural areas have, in the past, been provided mainly by farm labor representatives. These representatives have concentrated on meeting seasonal needs for farm laborers, coordinating the movements of migratory workers, and helping farmers to fill vacancies for year-round workers. They have also provided labor market information, which could guide farm workers in seeking other jobs, but have seldom gone beyond this in assisting displaced workers to move to nonfarm jobs or in meeting the needs of the much larger number of rural nonfarm workers and employers.[12]

In the early 1970s, a Rural Manpower Service was established in the U.S. Department of Labor, replacing the previous Farm Labor Service. This move was intended to broaden the role of the employment service in serving rural workers, especially by putting an end to the compartmentalization of services that tended to exclude nonfarm workers and employers. A recent evaluation of this effort concludes that:

> Although it has shifted its emphasis, the Rural Manpower Service clearly has a long way to go before it changes its employer-oriented image. There are many reasons why it had difficulty shifting to a rural manpower service, the most obvious of which is the power of agribusiness interests relative to both the Rural Manpower Service and the workers. The agency has few sanctions; it seeks primarily to promote employer use of the employment service, but its main sanction against the employer is to deny him the use of those services.
> Denial of the agency's services is a particularly impotent remedy when there are labor surpluses, or when labor market institutions have alternatives to the use of the employment service. Moreover, the narrow mission of the Farm Labor Service made it reasonably effective in meeting the employers' needs but made it very difficult to transform the Farm Labor Service's personnel and procedures into a true rural manpower service. Federal efforts in this direction are rendered even more difficult by the fact that the employment service has been controlled mainly by the states. Finally, farm workers' weaknesses make it difficult for them either to provide the necessary stimulus for change or to form an alternate constituency for the Rural Manpower Service.[13]

Because of the difficulties involved in creating more and better employment opportunities for rural people—and especially the poor and disadvantaged segments—the notion of *access* to opportunities needs to be developed in more detail. And to see best how access works one must look at cities rather than rural areas.

NOTES

[1] Don A. Dillman, "Population Distribution and People's Attitudes: Current Knowledge and Needed Research" (Paper prepared for the Urban Land Institute, October 15, 1973). See also Niles M. Hansen, *The Challenge of Urban Growth: The Basic Economics of City Size and Structure* (Lexington, Mass.: D.C. Heath and Co., Lexington Books, 1975), pp. 19–31.

[2] John Friedmann and John Miller, "The Urban Field," *Journal of the American Institute of Planners* 31, 4 (November 1965): 313–14.

[3] Ibid., p. 313.

[4] Brian J.L. Berry, "Spatial Organization and Levels of Welfare: Degree of Metropolitan Labor Market Participation as a Variable in Economic Development" (Paper presented to the Economic Development Administration Research Conference, Washington, D.C., October 9-13, 1967), p. 14.

[5] Ibid., p. 19.

[6] U.S. Department of Agriculture, Economic Research Service, *Characteristics of U.S. Rural Areas With Noncommuting Population,* prepared for the Senate Committee on Agriculture and Forestry, 92nd Cong., 2d sess. (Washington, D.C.: Government Printing Office, 1972).

[7] Ibid.

[8] Dale E. Hathaway, "A Public Employment Program for Rural Areas," *Federal Manpower Policy in Transition* (Washington, D.C.: Manpower Administration, U.S. Department of Labor, 1974), pp. 62–64.

[9] Ibid., p. 63.

[10] *Manpower Report of the President, 1971* (Washington, D.C.: Government Printing Office, 1971), p. 128.

[11] Ray Marshall, *Rural Workers in Rural Labor Markets* (Salt Lake City: Olympus Publishing Co., 1974), p. 132.

[12] *Manpower Report of the President, 1971,* p. 129.

[13] Marshall, p. 106.

Chapter Two

Geographic Disparities in Access to Economic Opportunities

URBANIZATION AND ACCESS

External Economies of Agglomeration

Increasing urbanization has characterized many advanced industrial countries for 200 years; today it is a worldwide phenomenon. Economic activities have been attracted to cities because of advantages associated with concentration and people have been drawn to them because they offer improved incomes and a diversity of employment and lifestyle options. Underlying the importance of access in cities is the notion of *externalities,* which have been defined as "the impacts of the activities of households, public agencies, or enterprises which are exerted otherwise than through the market. They are, in other words, relationships other than those between buyer and seller."[1] Originally the term *external economies* was used to denote the cost reductions experienced by individual firms in a growing industry. The relevant economies (service facilities, specialized education, etc.) were external to the firm but internal to the industry. More recently the term has come to be used to describe any economies of operation that are external to the firm but result from the previous presence of other firms (whether in the same industry or not) and social infrastructure such as roads, schools and utilities. External economies are therefore external to the firm but internal to the city or region.

From the perspective of the economist

a city is a dynamic system of interrelated and interdependent markets characterized by great density and specialization of economic actors as well as certain institutional conditions that influence decision making by many different governments, each of which has limited authority and competence. These markets serve and are served by large numbers of persons and firms located in relatively close proximity.[2]

It is the great proximity in cities that generates so many externalities. As Hirsch puts it, "the city is where externalities abound; and it is the prevalence of these externalities that make a city what it is."[3]

Harry Richardson has made a useful distinction among business, household and social external economies of agglomeration.[4] Business agglomeration economies include access to specialized business services; sources of capital; labor market economies in the form of more varied skills, greater elasticity of labor supplies, superior training and better organized worker placement services; a larger stock of managerial and professional talent; good public services; cultural amenities; opportunities for specialization because of the large market (product specialization, technical externalities, transport cost savings); economies of information and communication, especially where face-to-face contact is involved; greater adaptability and flexibility in the use of fixed capital; and last, but probably not least, the presence of a variety of business entertainment facilities (whose existence, it may be added, often depends on the liberal tax deductions allowed for business entertainment expenses).

Household agglomeration economies would include opportunities for earning higher incomes and a wide variety of jobs, shopping facilities, public services, leisure and cultural amenities, and housing. The efficient provision of major educational facilities, public transportation, hospitals, entertainment facilities and other types of social infrastructure usually requires some minimum population size threshold, though there may be a leveling off in many benefits in the medium size range.

Then there are the more nebulous *social agglomeration economies*. This refers to the functions performed by cities as centers of innovation, and their role in transmitting innovation through the urban hierarchy and to urban hinterlands. Wilbur Thompson has suggested that "[t]he large urban area would seem to have a great advantage in the critical functions of invention, innovation, promotion, and rationalization of the new. The stabilization and even institutionalization of entrepreneurship may be the principal strength of the large urban area."[5] In particular, the degree to which services, in the broadest sense, have become the real economic base of larger cities should be emphasized in this context.

> As we become more a service-oriented economy, the city itself becomes the very product that is being redesigned and re-engineered—becomes the experiment as well as the laboratory. Small wonder that the largest metropolitan areas can be so little concerned with promoting area industrial development, compared with the frantic activities of this kind conducted by the smaller areas.[6]

Innovation
The concentration of innovation in larger cities has been extended by Thompson into a more general theory of how industry that is born in large cities trickles down from them to smaller cities in the urban hierarchy.

Industries filter down through the system of cities, from places of greater to lesser industrial sophistication. Most often, the highest skills are needed in the difficult, early stage of mastering a new process, and skill requirements decline steadily as the production process is rationalized and routinized with experience. As the industry slides down the learning curve, the high wage rates of the more industrially sophisticated innovating areas become superfluous. The aging industry seeks out industrial backwaters where the cheaper labor is now up to the lesser demands of the simplified process.[7]

And it is of course small towns and rural areas that constitute the lowest rung of the filtering proc?. Thus, Thompson argues that a filter-down theory of industrial loca n goes far in explaining why the

smaller, less industrially dvanced area struggles to achieve an average rate of growth out of enlarging shares of slow-growth industries, which were attracted by the area's low wages. It would seem that both the larger industrial centers from which, and the smaller areas to which, industries filter down must run to stand still (at the national average growth rate); the larger areas do, however, run for higher stakes.

The economic development of the smaller, less developed urban area would seem to require that it receive each successive industry a little earlier in its life cycle, to acquire the industry at a point in time when it still has both substantial job-forming potential and high-skill work. Only by upgrading the labor force on the job and by generating the higher incomes (fiscal capacity) needed to finance better schools can the area hope to break out of its underdevelopment trap.[8]

My own studies of the spatial decentralization of industry to nonmetropolitan areas that have recently grown after previous stagnation or decline in population lends support to this position.[9] Nevertheless, it should be emphasized that we are talking here essentially about manufacturing decentralization and not about the decentralization of higher order tertiary activities; even though the latter may be decentralizing within metropolitan areas or shifting among metropolitan areas, there is relatively little movement to nonmetropolitan areas.

When discussing tertiary activities there may be a tendency to neglect the fact that the advantages of larger cities as centers of innovation are closely bound up with the production of information and communications. Information exchange for its own sake among specialists—for example, scientists—eventually raises the level of sophistication and technology in urban areas, and in consequence per capita income also will increase. A second kind of information exchange involves financial transactions between buyers and sellers who hope to benefit from it. Advertisements, sales personnel, brokers, inventories, catalogs, market research, phone calls and similar costs are incurred in order to facilitate the diffusion of knowledge about potential demanders and suppliers and their goods and services as well as the prices that can be expected to prevail.

Thus it appears that highly advanced postindustrialized urban economies are favored by extremely large amounts of pertinent information which, produced and exchanged at low cost, can greatly enhance the economy's efficiency. Under these conditions firms can make even fuller use of their entrepreneurial capacities, inventiveness, availability of capital, and access to new technology. Also, their knowledge of and access to resources, including labor, is improved, together with their understanding of today's and tomorrow's markets. Competition has been sharpened and so has the demand for product, production, distribution, and market innovation.[10]

In addition, it has been argued that no matter where a growth-inducing innovation takes place in the nation's system of cities, it is likely to appear soon in some or all of the largest cities. The latter would tend to adopt the innovation because of their "high contact probabilities" with many other places. Small places would tend to adopt late, if at all, because they have relatively few nonlocal goods and services transactions.[11]

Income
If agglomeration economies and innovations are the main propulsive mechanisms in the urban growth process, it should also be recognized that there is considerable evidence indicating that per capita income increases with city size—i.e., effective demand (purchasing power) present in the city grows at a faster rate than population.[12] Moreover, proximity to opportunities in other cities also is directly associated with per capita income. In a test of this relationship Alonso examined the influence of both absolute population size and the constellation of urban opportunities available to a person or a firm at a given location, on mean per capita income (1959), in metropolitan areas.[13] Considering that the analysis disregarded local resources; social, economic and political history; locational advantages; climate, and numerous other relevant variables, it was remarkable that these two variables alone accounted for better than one-fourth of the variance in per capita incomes. The conclusion to be drawn is that

it is misleading to consider only size, which is a measure of immediate opportunities, while neglecting the broader context of opportunities in other cities. Big and small must be qualified in their setting; whereas it may be quite good to be smaller in a dense setting, it may be necessary to be quite big in an isolated one. Policies of small and far, which are not uncommon, perhaps should be small and near, and big and far.[14]

The larger per capita income levels associated with larger city size or, more generally, with greater proximity to opportunities within the framework of the national system of cities are also associated with the attainment of numerous other goal variables. A study of 60 variables representing the full set of goals actually sought by metropolitan areas indicated that income indicators are the best single measures of overall goal attainment. If one were limited to specifying only a small number of goal dimensions, the goals which could not be subsumed under income would primarily be "physical" goals—e.g., purity of air and open space. Thus economic growth and physical planning are complementary aspects of efforts to attain generally accepted objectives associated with urban living.[15]

External Diseconomies

But can it be said that bigger is always better? Or at least better in terms of the foreseeable future? Unfortunately, the external economies that attract people and firms to cities are accompanied by their negative counterpart, external diseconomies, which are reflected in traffic congestion; air, water and noise pollution; social disorder; physical blight; high public investment requirements; and similar phenomena.

> The larger places have a clear and sizable advantage in such areas as cheaper and more flexible transportation and utility systems, better research and development facilities, a more skilled and varied labor supply, and better facilities for educating and retraining workers. Further, these economies of scale are captured by private business as lower private costs; at the same time private business is able to slough off on society various social costs that its presence imposes, such as its addition to traffic congestion and air pollution. If, then, the external diseconomies of business-created noise, dirt, congestion, and pollution are some increasing function of city size and/or density, factor market prices are biased in favor of large urban areas, and understate the true market costs of production in the metropolis. In the absence of sophisticated public management that would be needed to implement price reform, factor markets so biased promote urban growth and great size.[16]

Moreover, the argument that income per capita rises with city size could be interpreted to mean not only that larger cities are more productive, but also that firms that benefit from external economies do so only because they bribe workers to leave smaller—and presumably more satisfying—places by paying higher wages. If this is the case, it follows that (1) each worker relocates in keeping with his own trade-offs between money and psychological income and (2) the "extra" wage required to compensate workers for living in big cities is included in the costs of production in big cities.[17] When the goods and services produced in big cities are sold in the local market, the diseconomies are reflected in a higher cost of living. When they are exported, the purchasers bear the costs of these diseconomies, as they should. The market mechanism thus in part reflects the nonmarket costs and benefits of big city externalities; and to the extent that it does so it will promote upward pressure on big city wages or outmigration of workers who give relatively greater weight in their preferences to the nonmonetary psychological income of smaller places.

Despite the need for much more empirical evidence, there are indications that workers require monetary compensation to offset the negative externalities associated with large cities. Haworth and Rasmussen recently analyzed differences in the cost of living among metropolitan areas and found that although income does increase with city size, a substantial part of the differential may stem from cost of living differences. They conclude that "any discussion of optimum city size that uses money income will tend to overstate agglomeration economies and understate the relative well-being of nonmetropolitan areas."[18] This conclusion should probably be put this way: Agglomeration economies in large cities enable firms to compensate workers for negative externalities associated with such places, but in themselves they do not provide a sufficient argument in favor of large cities.

George Tolley has put together the results of a number of exploratory studies by other researchers and estimates that wage rates rise more rapidly with city size than do living costs. In his city of one million workers or four million people an average hourly wage rate of $4.00 contains an extra 5 percent—or 20 cents an hour—to compensate for negative externalities. In this city, Tolley estimates that the diseconomies of air pollution may be equivalent to 12.5 to 25 cents per working hour, and those of traffic congestion to 6 or 7 cents per working hour. The sum of these figures—18.5 to 32 cents per working hour—is about the same as the estimated 20 cent margin of wage rates over living costs. This margin may well then be a price paid to big city workers to offset big city negative externalities. Tolley concludes that:

> The results suggest the hypothesis that locational effects of externalities impinging on city residents are not negligible, but neither are they so large as to call for the dismantling of cities. A 5 percent increase in the cost of hiring labor would probably make a city grow less rapidly than otherwise, since many labor intensive firms on the margin between locating in the city and elsewhere would then find locations elsewhere more attractive. Since the large cities contain such a preponderance of the population, even a small effect in percentage terms on larger cities would greatly accelerate economic growth in rural areas.[19]

Wingo also has considered the impact of externalities on firms with different input cost structures and concludes that there is no reason to believe that externalities necessarily result in cities of larger than optimal size as long as labor and capital are mobile.[20] Moreover, from a national viewpoint, the optimum size of a city can only be defined within the context of the total national settlement pattern. As pointed out earlier, a small city with proximity to opportunities in large cities is likely to be better off in terms of most economic welfare indexes than a city of the same size located in a relatively isolated setting. But then the whole idea of an optimum size city per se has so few defenders that one wonders why anyone continues to feel an obligation to once more excoriate it.

Biases Favoring Metropolitan Growth

This is not to deny, however, that a city may be too big (or small) for some purposes. For example, there may well be biases that favor the growth of large cities at the expense of other places. For example, if blue collar, middle income workers may happen to prefer smaller towns or rural settings, this preference is likely to be negated by union pressures to equalize wages in all places. If wages are subject to national labor contracts then the location of firms is more likely to be influenced by management's preferences for urban amenities. The fact that an increasing number of managers show willingness to move corporate headquarters from the very largest cities—and especially New York—to other cities still should not provide much comfort for rural development advocates. The losses of the biggest will no doubt be the gain of the big.

Another bias in favor of large urban areas results from asymmetry in migration. The relatively young and better educated segments of the non-metropolitan population tend to move to big cities because of the attractiveness of their employment and lifestyle alternatives. However, "[w]ith time and aging, many come to favor the environment of smaller places, but the elderly tend not to move easily due to heavy sunk investments in homes, friends and local institutions and due also to the shorter remaining life over which the money and psychic cost of moving must be recaptured."[21] By simply not moving, many people in effect choose a larger place as a consequence of the long run growth of places that once were not large. Thus there is likely to be a bias in favor of bigness

> because those who prefer large cities do tend to act on those preferences and those who prefer smaller places tend not to act. Note also that this age-bias tends to reinforce the "skill-bias" in migration . . . through which professional and technical workers lock the semi-skilled production workers into their locational preferences for larger urban places.[22]

ACCESS IN NONMETROPOLITAN AREAS

Decentralizing Forces

Although some writers emphasize the importance of communications in promoting the growth of large cities, there also is a case to be made that in the electronic age it is no longer necessary for so many activities to cluster together in close proximity. New York-based RCA, one of the world's leading telecommunications firms, recently ran a national advertisement with the bold heading "Is New York Really Necessary?" The answer was an unequivocal "no." In this perspective most of the functions performed in downtown offices could just as well be done from homes; or if this is not yet the case, it could be if telecommunications technology were really turned loose. Moreover, many of the consumption amenities that were formerly only available in big cities are now available in the home. In cities where professional football games are being played many times more people watch the action in their living rooms than from the stands; even many ticket holders prefer to view the games at home. Pianist Glenn Gould maintains that the concert hall is a dead letter in the future; his performances are now limited to recordings. Of course there will always be people who want to experience cultural and entertainment activities directly, and for them only cities beyond a fairly large threshold size will do. Also, many people simply do not want to stay home all the time; preservation of the lifestyle associated with the tight-knit nuclear family seems not to have the attraction it once did. In any case, even though it is not difficult to see that innovations now originate in large cities or are rapidly picked up by them, one can readily envisage alternative work and residence patterns made possible by new communications technology. And these patterns may be just as productive, for the appropriate activities, as those now prevailing, and even more satisfying from the perspective of many households.

Obviously big cities are not going to wither, but their sizes and their structures are changing under the influence of technological, social and economic forces whose results are not always readily predictable. The growth rates of the largest SMSAs have been slackening spontaneously, and there is good evidence that many are now declining in population and more will in the foreseeable future.

Recent Population and Employment
Growth Patterns

It is particularly significant that in the period from 1970 to 1974 persons moving from SMSAs exceeded inmigrants from nonmetropolitan areas, according to Bureau of the Census survey-based estimates. The relevant data indicate that 5,965,000 persons four years old and over moved out of SMSAs while 4,121,000 moved in; in other words, there was a net migration loss from SMSAs to nonmetropolitan areas of 1,844,000.[23] Of course, this does not mean that SMSAs declined in population. Natural increase and immigration from foreign countries have been sufficient to maintain the long run trend of increasing urbanization of the American population. (Even during the decade of the 1960s only about one-ninth of total popula-

tion growth in SMSAs was a result of net inmigration from nonmetropolitan areas.) One interpretation of the net movement from SMSAs is that it
represents continuing urban development around the fringes of SMSAs.
During the 1960s jobs in the suburbs of SMSAs grew at a faster rate than
population. Because this trend no doubt has continued into the present
decade, workers can even more easily commute to these jobs from communities just beyond SMSA boundaries.

On the other hand, there is evidence that recent nonmetropolitan growth
is not simply a matter of the extension of urban (SMSA) fields. During the
1960s SMSA counties grew in population by 16.6 percent while nonmetropolitan counties were growing by only 4.4 percent. However, prelimi-
nary estimates of population change between 1970 and 1973 indicate that
SMSA counties grew by 2.2 percent, whereas nonmetropolitan counties
grew by 4.1 percent. Even more significant was the 3.7 percent growth rate
in counties not adjacent to SMSAs, since it indicates that these counties
grew more rapidly than SMSAs.[24] Employment data support these demographic findings. Data obtained nationwide from state employment security
office files show that from March 1970 to March 1973 there was an increase
of 7.8 percent in non-metropolitan-area jobs, but only a 3.6 percent increase in jobs located in SMSAs. Moreover, unlike the 1960s, when manufacturing was the only major industry group with a higher employment
growth rate outside SMSAs, the 1970 to 1973 estimates showed higher
nonmetropolitan growth in every component except government. Thus,
the trade and services sectors of small towns and rural areas have been
growing along with goods-producing activities.[25] In view of these and
related findings Calvin Beale has remarked that:

> Essentially every current trend in residential preferences, business loca-
> tion decisions, land use effects of affluence, closure of comparative differ-
> ences in facilities and amenities of rural and urban areas, and the end of major
> adjustments in extractive industries supports additional rural and small city
> growth. Some areas will become urban or metropolitan as a result of such
> growth, but this is normal. And it is always necessary to stress the great
> variation among rural areas in their prospects. But it is essential for policy-
> makers and the public in general to realize that the curve of rural and
> nonmetro population trends has inflected. The factors that impelled outmi-
> gration in the mid-century have lost most of their force. A new perspective is
> needed, both to understand the forces affecting rural development and the
> population consequences that result.[26]

Limitations on Decentralization
Despite this basically optimistic stance toward rural areas, Beale is no
Dr. Pangloss. He recognizes, for examples, that the energy crisis may be a
greater threat to rural areas than to the cities. The access that rural people

have to jobs and services often depends on the availability of relatively inexpensive fuel, and expectations with respect to travel time—which to many people is a more important factor than distance—will have to be altered if the 55 mph speed limit is enforced. In addition, the city dwellers use of nonmetropolitan America for recreation and second homes can be expected to decline as gasoline becomes rationed by means of coupons or the price system. This in turn may have adverse consequences for manufacturing related to these activities—e.g., mobile home, power boat and snowmobile firms, which have been among the most rapidly growing industries in rural areas.[27]

There also is some irony in the fact that the energy crisis has created something of a boom in rural extractive industries as the hunt for oil, gas and coal accelerates. World scarcities have meanwhile greatly increased the value of farm production and timber. But although these factors will have some retentive effect on the populations of farming, mining and forestry areas, the increase in primary sector employment will be far less than the increase in primary production because of continuing advances in labor-saving techniques. The basic dependence of rural people on secondary and tertiary sources of work will not be reversed.[28]

Of course, mere growth of secondary and tertiary employment in rural areas does not imply less need for manpower and human resource development programs in these areas. In the first place, industrial growth in rural hinterlands is by no means a universal phenomenon. And where it is occurring the sectors involved tend to be in the low wage, slow growth (and often heavily subsidized) class. Moreover, although tourism, recreation and related activities bring undoubted satisfactions to people who reside in metropolitan areas, as well as profit to many city-based developers, their positive impact on the local rural labor force is less certain. The tourist industry does not have strong linkages to other industries and usually does not lead to the growth of complementary activities. The kinds of skill required by the tourist industry are not those likely to lay the base for new industry; rather, what is usually needed are low level skills utilized in retail trade. It has been aptly remarked that "the promotion of tourism, while it may win political support from local chambers of commerce, dominated by the owners of retail establishments, is not likely to have much of a multiplier effect on the state economy such as the promotion of other industries is likely to have."[29]

FLIES IN THE RURAL GROWTH OINTMENT: THE CASE OF THE OZARKS

What has been termed the "largest and purist"[30] major rural area where population decline has been reversed recently is the Ozark-Ouachita region in Arkansas, Missouri and Oklahoma. It includes most of the Ozark Plateau and Ouachita Mountains, as well as the Arkansas River Valley in between. Here a contiguous group of 72 turnaround counties can be delineated. Although many rural development protagonists have called favorable attention to the growth of manufacturing and tourism and recreation activities in this area, it also represents a good example of the continuing need for rural manpower and human resource development programs.

The experience of the turnaround counties in the Ozarks conforms closely to the trickle-down theory of the spatial-temporal industrialization process. A study of rural industrialization and population growth in the area concludes that "the occurrence of low wage, labor intensive manufacturing in these rural counties raises the possibility that a 'filtering down' process suggested by Thompson may be occurring. That is, manufacturers who rely on the existence of pools of low wage, surplus labor are having to move on out of areas as the surplus disappears through competition with other, higher wage employers."[31] This process is not necessarily bad, because there is an implication that industry types, skills and wages will be upgraded in the long run. In fact this has happened in regions of the South which were among the first to gain substantial industry—e.g., the Piedmont Crescent, Georgia and, more recently, the Tennessee Valley.[32] But for now the situation in the Ozarks leaves much to be desired.

A recent study of 1413 households in towns with fewer than 2500 people and in the open country of the Ozarks region found that over half of the household heads were limited in their ability to work. One-third were age 65 or older, 14 percent were under 65 but disabled, 4 percent were able females under 65, and 2 percent were able persons under 65 with limited schooling. "Add to this the selective inmigration of people with values, aspirations, attitudes, and training similar to the native population, and the result is an increasingly limited labor force which attracts only low-wage, labor-intensive industry. When this happens the syndrome is only reinforced."[33] Thus, once economic poverty becomes concentrated in a region, the whole national system tends to operate so as to intensify that poverty, rather than to promote self-correction.

According to one theory consistent with findings in the rural Ozarks, the process of rural poverty ghettoization is related to the passing of values and attitudes conducive to economic poverty from parents to children. Bright and educated people move out, leaving disadvantaged people who have "adjusted" to their poverty situation. Low wage, low skill industries move in and attract other poverty-prone people into the region. Rural industrialization and vocational training will coexist with or even hasten poverty-generating processes because as better trained and educated persons leave they are replaced by less educated people. Transfer payments to the poor do little to change the fundamental causes of poverty. Economic stress results in less support for public facilities and services, resulting in adverse effects on the region's comparative advantage. At the same time there are strong pressures to condone environmental pollution and the exploitation of natural and human resources if it will keep the area's marginal firms in business. Unfortunately, the scholars who developed this rather grim picture of rural poverty in the Ozarks do not have very concrete policy proposals for dealing with the problems they identify. They find that "[t]he challenge to planners is to accept people's desires of where to live and to help build a better world in both rural and urban areas. The need is to adjust to people's preferences, not engineer them into a system they have rejected." Yet they admit that "[w]hat these people are willing to trade off for possible improvement hasn't been determined yet."[34]

There also is more than a hint here of rural fundamentalism, in the implied split between rural and urban areas. Given that urbanization is a fact of life—whether in terms of cities or the broader notion of urban fields—I am more inclined to favor the view set forth by former Arkansas governor Winthrop Rockefeller. Although he did not use the term, he argued that the future progress of regions like the Ozarks depends on the extension of urban fields. "There must be excellent *access* to the urban centers so that a mutually-supportive relationship can be cultivated—and a psychological identification and dependency between city and countryside established."[35]

SUMMARY AND CONCLUSIONS

All of the many problems of rural areas—and especially of poor rural areas—discussed in this and the previous chapter are related to access. The question is not simply one of getting rural people to move into or closer to metropolitan areas, but rather one of increasing the quantity and quality of opportunities available to rural residents in rural areas, as well as in cities to which some may commute. In many cases, rural-urban interdependencies may be strengthened, to the particular benefit of rural people, by the extension of urban fields from SMSAs. As pointed out in this chapter, this process is already at work in many areas all over the country, though decentralization around SMSAs may be impaired by a serious and prolonged energy crisis. In many other cases, however, rural counties will have to learn how to combine their forces to simulate the manpower and other services that are better developed in metropolitan labor markets. Innovative approaches will be required to increase access to opportunities through improved communications and information systems, more know-how in obtaining federal grants or in the effective use of revenue-sharing funds, and the sharing of complementary public facilities.

Rural areas are at a disadvantage not only because they lack sufficient labor market data, but also because they lack the personnel to prepare operationally feasible plans. As Hathaway points out,

> [m]ost, if not all, of the policy-making officials in the county or village government are part-time persons, skilled neither in government nor in manpower planning. These officials lack professional staff for planning purposes and they often are unaware of the existence of State and Federal programs which might fund pressing needs. Moreover, even if they know of such programs, they lack the expertise to fill out the applications and do the necessary followup work.[36]

It is not surprising that in summing up the findings of a conference on manpower services in rural America, Louis Levine stated: "It may well be that the greatest distinction between rural and metropolitan areas is in the differences in the public resource base—facilities, trained professional manpower, and adequate financing—and in the tradition of public service and social responsibility. Without these the delivery of manpower services can hardly become a reality."[37]

If many rural areas lack access to potentially valuable outside sources of information and funds, the haphazard nature of information about local rural labor markets differs from the situation in urban areas more in degree than in kind. In both cities and rural areas there exist marked deficiencies in this regard. They are the result of four major factors:

> (1) There is no formal mechanism by which data sources can be located, inventoried, and categorized. No systematic effort has been made, to our knowledge, to search out, develop, or build up an inventory of the major information resources in any local market.
>
> (2) Even for known data sources, there are no formal exchange and distribution procedures between interested parties. The occasional makeshift arrangements put together by one or two data users are a far cry from the needed formalization of policies, procedures, and major distribution channels for effective interchange.
>
> (3) There has been no careful analysis of the cost and benefits of a cooperative data-sharing program to the participants. A *quid pro quo* voluntary system, moreover, requires the identification of the major information needs, availabilities, and gaps of participants as its exchange foundation.
>
> (4) Among the many agencies and firms that would participate in a data-sharing program, there is no single institution clearly identifiable as the coordinator or clearing house for the system. A variety of coordinative functions, coupled with some procedural authority, would almost certainly be required at the hub of a local information system. Ideally, again, such a coordinating agency would be accepted voluntarily by all participants on the basis of its contribution to their individual needs. A search for means of overcoming these four major difficulties should, therefore, be the first order of business.[38]

If the past is any guide to the future, these difficulties will be overcome by an innovative program located in an SMSA. It may be hoped, however, that if the necessary innovations are not introduced in a rural area, the time required for them to diffuse to rural areas will be substantially less than might be expected under present conditions. On the other hand, the manpower planning landscape in rural areas is not entirely bleak. Among the brighter glimmers, some of which will be discussed in later chapters, one or more may, with appropriate encouragement, provide an example for emulation in urban as well as rural settings.

First, however, it is necessary to examine critically efforts that have been made in the last decade to improve access to employment opportunities for rural workers by promoting economic development in rural areas. Until recently most economists believed that the application of essentially Keynesian policy measures could be counted on to maintain reasonably full employment with reasonable price stability at the national level. Thus, with the Great Society programs of the 1960s there was a relative shift of official concern toward structural problems involving labor markets and the spatial distribution of resources. The former concern resulted in an unprecedented wave of manpower programs. The latter resulted in programs to help areas—primarily nonmetropolitan in nature—characterized by high unemployment and low income despite the high and rising level of national prosperity. The following chapter discusses the current status of growth center theory and practice because the growth center strategy has been adopted in principle in the major legislation concerning regional development. An evaluation of the major regional development policies actually implemented in the United States also is presented.

NOTES

[1] Ralph Turvey, "Side Effects of Resource Use," in Henry Jarrett, ed., *Environmental Quality in a Growing Economy* (Baltimore: Johns Hopkins Press, 1966), p. 47.

[2] Werner Z. Hirsch, *Urban Economic Analysis* (New York: McGraw-Hill, 1973), pp. 2–3.

[3] Ibid., p. xvi.

[4] Harry W. Richardson, "The Costs and Benefits of Alternative Settlement Patterns; Or Are Big Cities Too Big?" (Paper prepared for the United Nations Symposium on Population, Resources and Environment, Stockholm, September-October, 1973), pp. 14–15.

[5] Wilbur R. Thompson, "Internal and External Factors in the Development of Urban Economies," in Harvey S. Perloff and Lowdon Wingo, Jr., *Issues in Urban Economics* (Baltimore: Johns Hopkins Press, 1968), p. 53.

[6] Ibid., p. 54.

[7] Wilbur R. Thompson, "The Economic Base of Urban Problems," in Neil W. Chamberlain, ed., *Contemporary Economic Issues* (Homeword, Ill.: Richard D. Irwin, Inc., 1969), p. 8.

[8] Ibid., p. 9.

[9] Niles M. Hansen, *The Future of Nonmetropolitan America* (Lexington, Mass.: D.C. Heath and Co., 1973).

[10] Hirsch, p. 22.

[11] Allan R. Pred, "The Growth and Development of Systems of Cities in Advanced Economies" (Unpublished paper), p. 36.

[12] William Alonso, "The Economics of Urban Size," *Papers of the Regional Science Association* 26 (1971): 67–82.

[13] Ibid., p. 80.

[14] Ibid., p. 81.

[15] Robert E. Coughlin, "Attainment Along Goal Dimensions in 101 Metropolitan Areas," *Journal of the American Institute of Planners* 39, 6 (November 1973): 413–25.

[16] Thompson, "Internal and External Factors," p. 60.

[17] Lowdon Wingo, "Issues in a National Urban Development Strategy for the United States," *Urban Studies* 9, 1 (February 1972): 16–20.

[18] C.T. Haworth and D.W. Rasmussen, "Determinants of Metropolitan Cost of Living Variations," *Southern Economic Journal* 40, 2 (October 1973): 183–92.

[19] George S. Tolley, "Population Distribution Policy" (Paper presented at the Conference on Public Policy Education, Custer, South Dakota, September 11, 1971).

[20] Wingo.

[21] Wilbur R. Thompson, "The National System of Cities as an Object of Public Policy," *Urban Studies* 9, 1 (February 1972): 108.

[22] Ibid.

[23] U.S. Bureau of the Census, *Current Population Reports,* series P–20, no. 273, "Mobility of the Population of the United States: March 1970 to March 1974" (Washington, D.C.: Government Printing Office, 1974).

[24] The estimates were made by Calvin Beale. See William Chapman, "People Moving Back to Smaller U.S. Cities," *Washington Post,* October 27, 1974, p. A1.

[25] Calvin L. Beale, "Rural Development: Population and Settlement Prospects," *Journal of Soil and Water Conservation* 29, 1 (January-February 1974): 23–27.

[26] Ibid., p. 27.

[27] Ibid.

[28] Ibid.

[29] Alfred S. Eichner, *State Development Agencies and Employment Expansion* (Ann Arbor: University of Michigan and Wayne State University Institute of Labor and Industrial Relations, 1970), pp. 41–42.

[30] Beale, p. 26.

[31] Alfred W. Stuart, *Rural Industrialization and Population Growth: The Case of Arkansas* (Oak Ridge, Tenn.: Oak Ridge National Laboratory, 1971), p. 16.

[32] Hansen.

[33] Lloyd Bender, Bernal L. Green and Rex R. Campbell, "Ghettos of Poverty in the Ozarks," *Planning* 39, 7 (August 1973): 14.

[34] Ibid., p. 15.

[35] "Testimony of the Honorable Winthrop Rockefeller, Former Governor of Arkansas, to the Commission on Population Growth and the American Future, June 1, 1971" (Unpublished paper), p. 15. Emphasis added.

[36] Hathaway, p. 62.

[37] Louis Levine, "Conference Findings: Implications for Future Program Effectiveness," *Manpower Services in Rural America* (East Lansing: Michigan State University Center for Rural Manpower and Public Affairs, 1974), p. 198.

[38] Boris Yavitz and Dean W. Morse, with Anna B. Dutka, *The Labor Market: An Information System* (New York: Praeger, 1973), pp. 111–12.

Chapter Three

Growth Centers and Rural Development

INTRODUCTION

A leading manpower authority has written that

> [t]he essential economic problems of rural areas are to provide income or employment for the unemployed or underemployed, to upgrade work forces, and to facilitate the movement of people from labor surplus areas to other areas where jobs are more plentiful. Manpower programs could play an important role in both the process of industrialization and the movement of people to where job opportunities exist.[1]

Regional Policies

The regional development programs that have been implemented in the United States during the last decade have had objectives which are similar, though somewhat narrower in scope. They have attempted to improve income and employment opportunities for unemployed and under-employed persons, primarily in nonmetropolitan areas, and they have, in a very indirect and limited way, tried to promote labor mobility from labor surplus areas to "growth centers." However, only the Appalachian program has been directly involved in major human resource development programs, and, to a lesser extent, manpower programs.

Regional policy in the United States is primarily based on legislation passed in 1965, during the heyday of President Johnson's Great Society programs. There had, of course, been a number of prior experiments in regional development legislation. For example, during the 1930s such New Deal programs as the Tennessee Valley Authority, rural electrification and the Civilian Conservation Corps were based on public works and resource development and conservation. Following the Second World War a large number of local industrial development groups attempted to attract economic activity, but there were many more of these groups than there were new plants; moreover, many communities denied themselves badly needed public services in order to subsidize marginal firms. In the early part of the 1960s there was a renewal of interest at the federal level in helping "depressed areas." The Area Redevelopment Act of 1961 and the Accelerated Public Works Act of 1962 provided for public facilities in declining and stagnating communities. However, funds were not sufficient to overcome basic problems, planning was carried out on too small a scale and little attention was given to human resource development. Although a public works bias was carried over in the 1965 legislation, the two regional development acts passed in that year—the Appalachian Regional Development Act and the Public Works and Economic Development Act—represented an unprecedented attempt to deal with regional problems.

Growth Centers
Because of the potential efficiencies to be gained from external economies of agglomeration, these acts stated that investments should be concentrated in areas with significant growth potential. It was expected, or at least hoped, that public policy measures could induce growth in urban centers within or in proximity to economically lagging areas, and that eventually this growth would spread to the centers' hinterlands. In addition, hinterland workers could migrate or commute to the growth centers. Manpower and human resource issues were given little attention in the original major legislative acts, although the Appalachian program has evolved considerably in this regard.

Whatever one may make of the attempts to implement the growth center strategy, it still is called for in the relevant legislation. President Nixon's efforts, in 1974, to overhaul the present regional development institutional framework were in part based on complaints that there had not been enough concentration of investments in potential growth centers. Moreover, growth centers are still the topic of a large and rapidly expanding body of theoretical and empirical studies in economics, geography and related academic disciplines. For these reasons it is necessary to consider the current status of growth center theory and practice.

The first part of this chapter will reflect the fact that manpower issues have been neglected in most of the relevant technical literature, as well as in most national regional policies. In the experience of the United States this is particularly so in the case of the Economic Development Administration. Thus, its activities will be discussed in the more general context of this chapter. The experience of the Appalachian Regional Commission will be considered later, in the context of suggestions for more comprehensive approaches to rural problems—approaches involving manpower and human resource dimensions as well as measures to promote job creation.

Allowing for the fact that any significant body of knowledge or theory has numerous relevant historical antecedents, it may be stated with some confidence that the growth center literature originated two decades ago in the seminal works of Perroux, Hirschman and Myrdal.[2] In the mid-1960s I argued that while the growth center approach represented a substantial advance over both static location theory and the balanced growth and steady growth approaches, it nevertheless could not "be emphasized too much that the theory of development poles is badly in need of a thorough semantic reworking; the concepts and language which characterize it need more precise definition and more consistent usage. Even the notion of a development pole itself suffers in this regard."[3] In more recent years numerous critiques have sought to remedy this fault.[4] Most of these contributions have been valuable in their own right, but viewed as a whole they indicate that the growth center approach is still in a disordered state. Nevertheless, despite genuine difficulties that have arisen from particular empirical and theoretical contexts, major themes of the growth center literature still have relevance to regional policy.

SPONTANEOUS AND INDUCED GROWTH

It has been alleged that some of the difficulty has come about because the growth center label has been attached to different concepts, but that "[i]ntroduction of William Alonso's and Elliott Medrich's useful categorization of growth centers as *spontaneous* or *induced* appears to resolve the conflict."[5] In their scheme, induced growth centers are those in which public policy is trying to promote growth; there is a normative element in the designation of a locality as a growth center. Spontaneous growth centers, in contrast, are growing without the benefit of special assistance, or at least without the benefit of conscious or explicit policy.[6]

At this point it must be emphasized that the growth center literature largely originated as a response—or better, a reaction—to the deductive models of classical location theory, as well as to highly simplified and abstract models of economic growth. The growth center approach was supposed to be more oriented toward immediate policy issues, in particular the overconcentration of people and economic activity in one or a few large urban areas and problems of stagnation or decline in some nonmetropolitan areas. Moreover, it has obvious relevance to efforts to bring about "concentrated decentralization," a strategy which, it has been widely felt, "will surely prove more effective in promoting various development goals than would either entirely dispersing growth or entirely concentrating it in very large cities."[7]

In view of these considerations there can be no doubt that the growth center approach was primarily concerned with induced growth centers, as means both for slowing the growth of one or more spontaneous growth centers and for promoting growth in other areas. More recently, however, this normative concern has tended to give way to positive approaches related primarily to spontaneous growth centers. Thus, one of the most recent major contributions to the literature limits its emphasis explicitly to "natural growth poles."[8] While there is of course nothing wrong per se with positive analyses of spontaneous growth centers, they do shift the ground from the major issues that originally were the major raison d'être for the growth center notion.[9] The point is not that spontaneous growth centers should be neglected, but rather that a great deal of sterility can be avoided by viewing them in a policy context.

It is somewhat ironic that I have been accused of neglecting induced growth centers in favor of studying spontaneous growth centers,[10] because I proposed a growth center strategy for the United States based on spontaneously growing intermediate-size cities. My major point, however, was that it appears economically rational to accelerate (induce) growth in such places because they have more opportunities in terms of existing external economies than do smaller towns and rural areas and fewer diseconomies than do the largest cities. The accelerated growth of intermediate centers would be made conditional on the granting of newly created employment opportunities to a significant number of workers from lagging regions who could either commute or migrate.[11]

Similarly, the distinction between spontaneous and induced growth centers made by Alonso and Medrich was not intended to shift emphasis from normative to positive considerations. Rather, they argued that spontaneous growth centers should be studied "both for the lessons they may hold for inducing growth where it does not occur spontaneously and for their own sake as a valid subject of national developmental policy, since growth also has its problems."[12]

GROWTH CENTERS, CENTRAL PLACES AND THE URBAN HIERARCHY

Evolution of Growth Center Theory

Although growth center theory began in large part as an attempt to grasp the complex technical origins and dynamic interrelations of the growth process, expositions of the theory were generally presented in an input-output framework, usually in terms of a regionalization of the basic Leontief-type model, or by applying modifying vectors or matrixes to the basic model. Unfortunately it was frequently not possible to quantify the modifying variables. Thus, while some contributions were made to operationally meaningful theory, an approach that was supposed to deal with the polarization *process* in fact dealt largely with static effects.[13] Other elements in early works included such well-known analytic devices as location coefficients, simple graph theory and shift-share breakdowns of employment change.

Eclecticism continues to characterize the growth center literature, but with a relative shift in emphasis. The early seminal works were written by economists and emphasized economic variables, economic relations and economic growth. In the past decade geographers—and economists more interested in location theory than in growth—have entered the lists in increasing numbers and it may properly be said that their studies have, for a time at least, dominated the field. In consequence, less weight has been given to economic analysis and more to relationships of growth centers to central place theory and city size distributions. The positive side of this phenomenon is that greater attention has been focused on the "where" of economic activity, which is of course what regional economic policy is about. On the other hand, it also represents something of a return to the static approaches against which the original growth center writers were reacting. I say "something of a return" because this literature is not limited to static-descriptive studies of central places and urban hierarchies. It significantly adds dynamic notions of filtering and spread within urban systems. Before examining this point further it would be instructive to note the generally ambiguous empirical role of central place hierarchies.

City Size Distributions
Berry, for example, has found that "[t]here are no relationships between type of city size distribution and either relative economic development or the degree of urbanization of countries, although urbanization and economic development are highly associated."[14] Von Böventer has convincingly argued on theoretical grounds that satisfactory economic growth as well as the personal well-being of a country's citizens are compatible with wide differences in the degree of spatial concentration of population and economic activity. Particular rank-size distribution parameters are no help in national planning decision processes.[15] In a somewhat narrower vein, it has been shown that the central place schemes of Christaller and Lösch, with their concentration on market-oriented functions, contain restrictive assumptions which render them "inadequate as a general theoretical framework for analyzing the diffusion of growth, especially in the case of highly developed economies."[16]

Innovations, Economic Activities and the
Urban System
Nevertheless, by relaxing the assumptions of the classical approaches, a central place model can be used as a kind of landscape in which development-related diffusion processes operate.[17] This appears to be what Berry has in mind when he maintains that there are two major

elements in the way in which economic activities in space are organized around the urban system.[18] The first is a hierarchical system of cities, arranged according to the functions performed by each city; the second is a corresponding set of urban areas of influence (urban fields) surrounding each of the cities in the system. What Berry terms "impulses of economic change" have, he finds, been transmitted simultaneously in the system along three planes: first, outward from heartland metropoli to those in large regional hinterlands; second, from higher to lower urban centers in the hierarchy, in a pattern of hierarchical diffusion; and third, outward from urban centers into their surrounding urban fields in the form of radiating spread effects, of which more will be said in the following section. In this context modern growth theory, as described by Berry, would suggest that:

> continued urban-industrial expansion in major metropolitan regions should lead to catalytic impacts on surrounding areas. Growth impulses and economic advancement should filter and spread to smaller places and ulti- mately infuse dynamism into even the most tradition-bound peripheries. Growth center concepts enter the scene if filtering mechanisms are perceived not to be operating quickly enough, if "cumulative causation" leads to growing regional differentials rather than their reduction . . . or if institu- tional or historical barriers block diffusion processes. The purpose of spatially-selective public investments in growth centers, it is held, is to hasten the focused extension of growth to lower echelons of the hierarchy in outlying regions, and to link the growth centers more closely into the national system via higher-echelon centers in the urban hierarchy.[19]

This position is consistent with the contention that "the role played by growth centers in regional development is a particular case of the general process of innovation diffusion," and that therefore "the sadly deficient 'theory' of growth centers can be enriched by turning to the better developed general case."[20] Yet this approach is not without its own am- biguities. For example, modern growth theory asserts that within urban- regional hierarchical systems "impulses of economic change are transmit- ted in order from higher to lower centers in the urban hierarchy," so that "continued innovation in large cities remains critical for extension of growth over the complete economic system."[21] There is considerable evidence that the advantages which larger cities have as centers of innova- tion are closely bound up with the production of information and communi- cations.[22] In addition, it has been argued that no matter where a growth- inducing innovation takes place in the nation's system of cities, it is likely to appear soon in some or all of the largest cities because of the high contact probabilities which the latter have with many other places.[23] However, it is one thing to say that large cities are prime candidates to adopt innovations made in smaller centers, and quite another to say that innovation *in* large cities is critical, and that the transmission process works only in order from higher to lower centers.

Moreover, it is not always clear what is being transmitted through the urban hierarchy. For example, in certain of his earlier general discussions, Berry seems to break away from the confines of that concentration on market-oriented functions which, as Parr correctly points out, make the central place approach inadequate as a general theoretical framework for analyzing the diffusion of growth. In this broader context Berry talks about the transmission of rather general entities such as "innovations" or "impulses of economic change." But in attempting empirical verification of his argument, he has given prominent attention to the diffusion of television stations and sets—an extremely market-oriented phenomenon.[24] Similarly, in developing a growth center strategy for the Upper Great Lakes he leaned heavily on the hierarchy of market-oriented central places in the region (metropolis, wholesale-retail center, complete shopping center, partial shopping center, convenience center).[25] Again, apart from television diffusion, one searches in vain here for concrete examples of the transmission of specific "innovations" and "impulses of economic change."

To summarize, it would appear that reliance on a traditional, market-oriented hierarchy of central places scheme does not provide an adequate growth model. On the other hand, if one is concerned with innovations and impulses of economic change, using the central place model as a locational matrix or landscape, it should be recognized that "information can be exchanged between centers of the same size; innovations can be diffused laterally within the hierarchy (i.e., between centers of the same level); the diffusion process can even operate in an upward direction, as opposed to the more likely downward direction."[26]

As pointed out later in this chapter, more recent studies by Pred, Törnqvist and Goddard indicate that these issues may be clarified by shifting the focus of attention to organizational information flows within urban systems. In any case, it is clear that urban and regional growth issues need to be viewed in the context of the national urban system, even though it is premature to be overly doctrinaire about the nature of the precise functioning of dynamic processes within the system.[27]

Intermediate Size Cities

Without wishing to appear doctrinaire myself, I might add that a recent critique of the role of central place hierarchies in growth center studies still leaves open the issue of the feasibility of a policy based on intermediate size cities.

> The welter of confusion in relation to the actual functioning of central place processes tends to undermine discussions on the relevance of size

requirements for growth poles which are expected to coexist within a system of cities. If development stimuli can be motivated up and down the structural hierarchy at will, then the development-pole centre requirement is condensed to a provision of a centre capable of establishing strong linkages, regardless of size or position in the hierarchy. The policy advocated by Hansen for intermediate centres to act as development poles is not without merit. These centres will continue to stimulate the development of backward linkages at a subregional level, while building up the market thresholds that provoke forward linkages to cluster upon them. Extremes of pole planning at the highest and lowest orders of the urban hierarchy will be avoided, and the resultant centre may be able to stimulate development within an adjacent depressed region (unlike the cross-hierarchy linkage national centre), as well as providing a suitable base for agglomeration economies (unlike subregional centres).[28]

Here, however, it is necessary to give more careful attention to the role of growth centers as stimulators of development within their hinterlands. While no student of urban and regional economics would deny the importance of agglomeration economies, it is by no means clear that the growth they help to generate in urban centers results in beneficial spread effects for surrounding lagging areas. The experience of the Economic Development Administration illustrates this point.

THE ECONOMIC DEVELOPMENT ADMINISTRATION GROWTH CENTER APPROACH

The Scope of EDA Activities

EDA was created by the Public Works and Economic Development Act (PWEDA) to assist multistate regional commissions and to provide assistance in its own right to areas experiencing chronic economic distress. Eligibility for EDA assistance is based on one or more of the following general economic conditions: (1) a substantial or persistent unemployment level for an extended period of time, (2) a median family income at a level of less than 40 percent of the national level and (3) an actual (or prospective) abrupt rise in unemployment resulting from the closing of a major employer.

To implement its development goals EDA has at its disposal a wide range of program tools, including grants and loans for public works and development facilities; industrial and commercial loans; and an extensive program of technical, planning and research assistance. As of June 30, 1973, EDA reported that it had approved 3008 public works projects amounting to nearly $1.44 billion. About half of these expenditures were for water and sewer projects. There were 413 approved business development projects involving $326.7 million in loans and $65.6 million in working capital. A total of $93.8 million was provided for technical assistance and $44.2 million for planning grants. All programs together received $1.90 billion. California received the most money—$135 million. However, six of the seven next highest recipients were Southern states. The seven were Mississippi ($96 million), Kentucky ($89 million), Pennsylvania ($72 million), Texas ($71 million), Tennessee ($69 million), Georgia ($68 million) and West Virginia ($68 million).

In addition to regional commissions, the PWEDA called for three other categories of institutions for dealing with regional development problems. "Redevelopment areas" include counties, labor areas and certain cities where unemployment and low incomes require particularly urgent assistance. "Economic development districts" are multicounty organizations within which counties and communities work cooperatively on mutual needs and opportunities. "Economic development centers" are communities or localized areas with fewer than 250,000 persons where resources are to be used rapidly and effectively to create more jobs and higher incomes for the population of the surrounding area. Although these growth centers need not be within depressed areas, they are intended to promote economic development in redevelopment areas within the districts of which the centers and redevelopment areas are a part.

Critique of Growth Center Strategy

Early in its existence EDA experimented with a "worst first" strategy whereby areas with the most severe difficulties in each category of aid eligibility were to receive top priority for funds from the agency. The worst first strategy, in so far as it was implemented, was inconsistent with the notion of clustering investments in the growth centers of EDA districts. On the other hand, EDA's experience with the growth center approach has left much to be desired. For example, an evaluation carried out within the agency itself concludes that:

> EDA's experience in funding projects in economic development centers has not yet proven that the growth center strategy outlined in the Agency's legislation and clarified in EDA policy statements is workable. The Agency's approach to assisting distressed areas through projects in growth centers has resulted in minimal employment and service benefits to residents of depressed counties.[29]

Of course, this lack of success does not necessarily mean that a growth center strategy would not be workable. It may rather reflect the nature of the centers selected by EDA. Brian Berry has pointed out that:

examination of the gradients of influence of smaller centers indicates clearly that there seems little sense in trying to use small urban places as growth centers—their regional influence is too limited. Indeed, very few cities of less than 50,000 population appear to have any impact on their regional welfare syndrome, although admittedly the few that do are located in the more peripheral areas.[30]

The growth centers that have been designated by EDA are generally smaller than this 50,000 population level. As of April 15, 1970, there were 87 EDA-designated economic development districts with 171 development centers (126 economic development centers and 45 redevelopment centers; the latter were in redevelopment areas whereas the former were not). Only 30 of the development centers had a population greater than 50,000 and only 13 had a population greater than 100,000. Forty-two of the centers had fewer than 10,000 persons. Moreover, between 1960 and 1970, 61 percent of these development centers had population growth below the national average; 38 percent of the development centers—and over half of the redevelopment centers—experienced population declines.

General dissatisfaction with EDA also was reflected in President Nixon's proposal to Congress for an Economic Adjustment Act to restructure federal programs for area and regional economic adjustment. The initial report in this regard reaffirms the notion that "priority should be given to those areas with the greatest potential of providing higher productivity jobs for the underemployed, rather than attempting to create more productive jobs in all areas of high underemployment."[31] The report also is sharply critical of EDA's past performance.

> The policy of dispersing assistance rather than focusing on those [areas] with the greatest potential for self-sustaining growth has resulted in much of EDA's funds going to very small communities. Over a third of its public works funds have gone to towns with less than 2,500 people, and over a half to town with less than 5,000 population. There are relatively few kinds of economic activities which can operate efficiently in such small communities, so the potential for economic development in the communities is relatively small.[32]

GROWTH CENTER RATIONALE

The question remains: What would have happened if EDA outlays had been concentrated in larger centers? Would the basic rationale for the strategy have produced positive results in terms of center growth and spread effects if larger centers had been used? Before examining relevant evidence, the rationale itself can be briefly presented by reference to Figure 3–1, which shows a "typical" EDA multicounty district containing a mix of

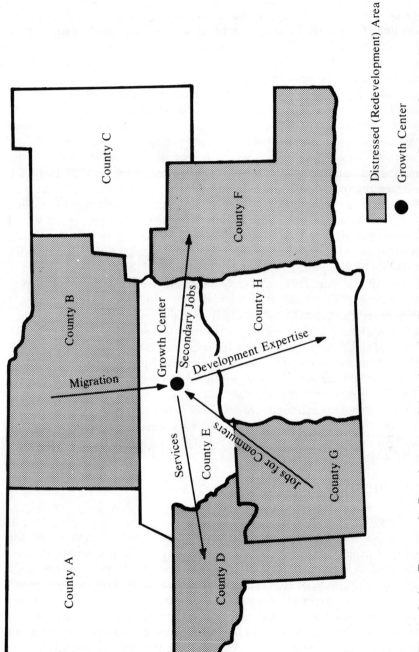

Figure 3-1. Economic Development Administration Development District and Growth Center Concepts.

distressed and relatively healthy counties. Ideally, the growth center's hinterland benefits from the spread of services, secondary jobs and development expertise from the center, as well as from opportunities made available to hinterland residents who commute or migrate to the core. It may be noted that what one chooses to call a spread effect often depends on the particular perspective of the viewer. For example, from the perspective of County B in Figure 3–1, it is not clear that migration will be beneficial, whether the migrants go to the growth center in County E or leave the district altogether. If the migrants were unemployed *or* if unemployed workers with similar skills can replace the employed workers who migrate the total output of County B would not or should not fall. Because the unchanged output is now divided among fewer people in County B, the average real per capita income will be higher than before. This may be regarded as a spread effect. On the other hand, the emigration of skilled workers who were employed in County B (or for whom employment would soon be found), and who were earning an income higher than the county average would result in a decline (or prevent as high a rise as otherwise possible) in the average real per capita income of the people remaining in County B and would also adversely affect the overall skill composition of its economy. This would be a backwash effect, in Myrdal's terminology.[33] Of course, if migrants from County B go to the district growth center they may spend more of their earnings in County B than if they had migrated to more distant places. The leakage from County E would benefit County B but would obviously not affect the district. Finally, apart from these economic considerations, there are those of a political and social nature. Outmigration is often regarded as undesirable by people living in an area, whether or not the economic consequences are desirable for the people left behind. Here, too, the results would vary depending on whether one adopted the perspective of a single county, a single district or a geographically wider frame of reference.

THE QUESTION OF SPREAD EFFECTS

Empirical Evidence

The notion of spread effects is most commonly associated with the induced generation of "secondary jobs" in hinterland counties such as County F in Figure 3–1. This is largely because of a pronounced tendency to identify the induced effects of an economic activity with *locally* induced effects. However, the great weight of the empirical evidence indicates this view to be mistaken. For example, Beyers' analysis of interindustry purchases and sales relationships in the Puget Sound region found that regional interindustry connections were weak compared to interregional interindustry relations. Value added and personal consumption were the most important regional linkages for many sectors. His data "suggest that Perroux's conceptualization of a growth pole, with its heavy emphasis on growth stimuli being transmitted via forward and backward interindustry linkages, is probably more applicable at a broad national level than at the small regional scale."[34] Gaile's growth center test of the Milwaukee area led to the finding that "the concept of concentric 'spread' of growth from the 'growth center' has not been proven."[35] In another paper, Gaile reviewed 17 studies using the growth center concept and concluded that if a trend was discernable it was that spread effects were either smaller than expected, limited in geographic extent or less than backwash effects.[36] A study by Gray of the employment effect of a major new aluminum reduction and rolling mill at Ravenswood, West Virginia, 50 miles north of Charleston, found that the induced employment attributable to the plant's operations could be traced mainly to Ohio (power) and Louisiana (bauxite), but very little was discernible around Ravenswood.[37]

Investing in Hinterlands

There is even a case to be made for investing directly in hinterland areas on the ground that such outlays might benefit "growth centers" as much as the hinterlands. Nichols' analysis of the propulsive effect of growth poles suggests that investments be concentrated in towns with the strongest linkages to hinterlands, but if these linkages are weak, as the foregoing evidence would indicate, "there are also advantages to be gained from injecting capital in lower order centres, or even the agricultural base, because increases in incomes in these places will generate strong income multipliers in higher order centres but not the other way round."[38] Moseley's studies of the spatial impact of Rennes, France, and of spatial flows in East Anglia also cast doubt on the notion that spatial concentration of investment will inevitably benefit much wider geographic areas. He concludes that "given an objective to foster the economic development of a number of small towns in a region, then direct investment in those towns would appear to be required. 'Trickle down' cannot be relied on. If 'some growth' is required throughout an urban hierarchy, then there is a case of neglecting the larger settlements to which some 'trickle up' might normally be expected."[39]

Conclusions

In the light of this evidence it would be difficult to justify growth center policies for lagging areas on the basis of spread effects. This is not to say that cities in general do not generate spread effects. Clearly larger cities do in urban systems where one or two cities are not in a position of unmistakable dominance;[40] the problem is that larger cities are rarely found in lagging regions.[41] However, the case for growth center strategies aimed at helping people in lagging areas does not necessarily depend on the spread effect justification. If it can be shown that large numbers of potentially mobile persons in lagging areas would *prefer* to move to intermediate-size growth centers rather than stay at home or move to large metropolitan areas, the case for settlement pattern strategies oriented toward the development of intermediate-size cities would be reinforced. There has been very little research in this regard, but findings based on surveys in the United States indicate that such preferences do in fact exist.[42]

Of course, not everyone can or should leave lagging regions, because of the profound historical, social and political realities which must necessarily temper policies based on economic criteria. Fortunately, some of these regions have benefited and will benefit from the extension of urban fields and the decentralization of manufacturing.[43] But these phenomena will not automatically solve the problems of all lagging areas. While some consideration might be given to the promotion of smaller growth centers, provided they have genuine growth potential, the principal focus of policies for lagging areas should be on the development of service centers oriented toward upgrading human resources and the quality of life. Improved health, education and other service delivery systems are likely to result in increased migration to places with greater economic opportunity. This should be viewed as a social gain rather than a cause for alarm, at least in so far as regional policy aims at increasing individual welfare rather than maintaining or expanding the number of persons resident in a given area. In the long run, however, outmigration may be expected to decline. Many persons who benefit from social investments will choose to remain in lagging regions because of attachment to family, friends, surroundings, etc. These persons eventually will constitute a body of qualified labor sufficient to justify increased public infrastructure development and expanded directly productive activities. This general approach probably would not produce dramatic short run changes (a political liability), but it would permit a gradual adaptation of regional population to regional resources.

In summary, then, while it is difficult to justify economically a growth center strategy on the basis of spread effects, this is not the case for a strategy based on the expansion of economic infrastructure and directly productive activities in intermediate-size cities, coupled with emphasis on improved human resource development systems in lagging regions. Admittedly, though, attempts at implementing such a strategy would meet with political resistance—e.g., from politicians losing constituents in lagging regions and from ''no growth'' advocates in intermediate growth centers.

DIRECTIONS FOR GROWTH CENTER RESEARCH

Lack of a Unifying Theory

The immediately foregoing analysis would suggest that less emphasis be placed in growth center research on the delineation of urban hierarchies and central place schemes, and more on the costs and benefits associated with various types of public and private investments in various city sizes (taking account also of cities' access to opportunities in other areas, which can be estimated with gravity models), and on the nature and significance of people's location preferences.

More generally, I would argue that the lack of a unifying theory in growth center research is attributable primarily to its ambitious scope; it is no simple task to bind together such concepts and issues as the roles of external economies and diseconomies, economies of scale, regional and urban growth thresholds, propulsive sectors and their multiplier effects, interindustry linkages, growth transmission in spatial terms, migration and commuting patterns, and the induced and inducing nature of public investment. Some writers even urge that "psychological polarization" is a key element in the growth of both industry and tourism.[44] The fact that no one has succeeded in combining all these factors within the framework of an operationally feasible model should not rule out efforts to build from more modest bases.

Innovation Diffusion
It was pointed out earlier that growth center analysis was supposed to provide a dynamic alternative to static location models. Yet the French school of regional economists tended to fall back on static models. More recently, geographers have shed valuable light on spatial diffusion of innovation processes, though sometimes within the framework of rather rigid, market-oriented hierarchical central place schemes. Thomas represents a notable exception in this regard. Building from the work of Perroux and Hirschman, he has emphasized the *economics* of why, how and where a growth center grows, and he has convincingly urged that specific industry growth patterns need to be examined for clues to improving our conceptual framework for dealing with the disequilibria of propulsive industries, internal and external economies, technological change and productivity growth, innovation, and the diffusion of new techniques.[45] Fortunately, this work has been extended in range and depth by numerous researchers involved in the University of Washington's Growth Pole and Regional Development Project.[46]

Lasuén has also made important contributions toward the elaboration of a dynamic growth center theory based on the complex interaction between economic growth and spatial organization. He begins, like Thomas, with the work of Perroux and attempts to reorient growth center theory by developing a neglected but essential hypothesis of Perroux.

Following Schumpeter's lead, Perroux stated that economic development results from the adoption of innovations; then extending Schumpeter's view, Perroux implicitly advanced the main hypothesis that innovations in several subsidiary lines will follow in the wake of an innovation in a dominant industry, and that these innovations would be located in geographical clusters around the same industry.[47]

Lasuén recognizes the value of central place theory in helping to understand service activity location,

> [b]ut for the explanation of the evolution of the system of cities we need the growth pole approach, for no other framework is as well fitted to explain why and how the newer activities will come about and locate. Thus, it can easily be hypothesized that the present system of poles is the result of the impact of a past system of innovations and that newer systems of poles will be brought about by newer systems of innovations.[48]

In Lasuén's analytic framework economic development results from the adoption of successive packages of innovations in dominant industries. Moreover, these sectorially clustered sets are also geographically clustered. Functional and spatial impacts produce disturbances in the sectorial and geographic distribution of activities. The diffusion and adoption of successive sets of innovations follow similar patterns, resulting in a fairly stable system of poles. Over time successive innovations demand greater scales of operation and larger markets; they also come at shorter intervals. Larger cities are the earliest adopters of innovations, which then diffuse gradually to the rest of the urban system. As a consequence of this process, the system of growth poles becomes increasingly hierarchic in nature.[49]

Lasuén also insists on the importance of business organization in the polarization process. If innovation diffusion is delayed because of inadequate organizational arrangements, then appropriate changes need to be made in order to minimize the costs and risks inherent in the learning process.

> At present, the emphasis of development policies (national, regional, and local) is placed on production. Policies are geared to promote producers. According to our analysis the emphasis should be placed on marketing and technical know-how. The provision of facilities warranting complete commercialisation of the products: commercial credit, publicity, marketing sales-servicing, etc. and of the know-how required to start a smooth and standardised production—via licensing contracts, custom manufacturing agreements or technical assistance and research and development programmes, is a round about but most effective way of guaranteeing the promotion of specific productions.[50]

Lasuén reaches an extreme of audacity among urban economists when he proposes that the adoption of innovations in industry and services could be furthered by learning from the experience of agricultural extension programs, and particularly from the way in which they have reduced the risks of adopting agricultural innovations.[51]

Business Organization and Information Flows

Emphasis on business organization also characterizes important recent efforts by geographers to analyze the nature and significance of information flows for the urban system. Pred, for example, argues that if policymakers wish to reduce regional employment inequalities, and if they wish to provide new jobs that do not require outmigration from rural areas, they should take two coordinated measures. These would be:

1) to promote urban production and *administrative* activities which not only will give rise to regional exports, but *intra*regional urban interdependencies as well; and

2) to improve air or other communications between the existing cities selected for the location of new activities, and between those locations and major metropolitan centers elsewhere in the country. That is, insofar as possible large non-local multipliers ought be internalized within the target region and concentrated at a limited number of spatially dispersed cities that are made more accessible to one another in terms of the ease of making face-to-face organizational contacts. This should not only mean more new jobs in the short-run. To the extent that new functional linkages and communications possibilities generate spatial biases in the availability of specialized information, the two steps should improve long-run development prospects by increasing subsequent probabilities both for the intraregional diffusion of growth-inducing innovations and for the organizational selection of intraregional operational decision-making alternatives. On the other hand, if intraregional urban interdependencies are not created, and if interurban communications are not improved, the short-run multipliers and long-run employment benefits will leak out of the region to an unnecessary degree, mostly to major metropolitan areas located in other regions.[52]

Pred further suggests that policies aiming at concentrated decentralization should

create new interdependencies between selected small metropolitan areas, regardless of whether or not they are located in the same broadly defined region. In particular, if the policy is to increase its probability of long-run success through circular and cumulative feedbacks, some high-level organizational administrative activities—with their characteristically high local multipliers—should be among the activities located at the decentralization foci. The artificially created interdependencies associated with such a policy would, in turn, require improved air connections between the selected "intermediately-sized" cities so as to facilitate the non-local face-to-face exchange of non-routine specialized information. Thus, to take a totally hypothetical example, if Fresno, California, and Chattanooga, Tennessee— two cities in Hansen's suggested 200,000–750,000 population range—were among a small set of cities designated as "intermediately-sized" growth centers, it would be necessary to subsidize or create frequent non-stop air service between them and thereby eliminate time-costly plane transfers at San Francisco, Atlanta, or some other intervening large metropolitan area.[53]

Goddard, in a synthetic study based on evidence concerning information flows in Great Britain, the United States and Sweden, derives similar policy conclusions.[54]

Increasing research on information flows obviously is relevant to the significance attached to access in the last chapter; moreover, it is serving to correct an unjustly neglected area in the growth center literature. Yet the emphasis given to the functioning of the "postindustrial society" should not detract from the opportunities that manufacturing decentralization represents for many rural areas. In fact, better access within national communications networks can be of considerable help to rural areas not only in attracting more manufacturing activity, but in upgrading its quality. This in turn depends on the ability of rural people to take advantage of opportunities—i.e., on the quality of rural human resources. The failure of most growth center theory and practice to include explicitly human resource and manpower dimensions is at least equal to the neglect of information circulation. One notable exception in the realm of regional policy is the Appalachian program.

APPALACHIAN GROWTH CENTERS AND HUMAN RESOURCES

Scope of the Appalachian Program

The Appalachian Regional Development Act (ARDA) established the Appalachian Regional Commission (ARC) for the purpose of coordinating a six year (since extended) joint federal-state development effort—the largest such program yet undertaken in the United States. ARC maintains that its social goal is to provide the people of Appalachia with the health and skills they require to compete for opportunity wherever they choose to live. The economic goal is to develop in Appalachia a self-sustaining economy capable of supporting the people with rising incomes, improving standards of living and increasing employment opportunities.

The Appalachian program involves 13 states—stretching from north-eastern Mississippi to southern New York—but the only whole state included is West Virginia. Given this vast expanse of territory it is not surprising that ARC itself distinguishes "four Appalachias," each with its own needs and potentials. The ARDA gave ARC a broad range of functions and a more narrow set of programs to administer, as well as general guidelines for these purposes. ARC was given specific program and funding authority in nine functional areas: health, housing, vocational education, soil conservation, timber development, mine restoration, water survey, water and sewer facilities, and highways. The commission also was given supplemental grant authority and provided with program funding linkages to local development districts.

Strictly speaking, ARC is not a federal agency, but rather, a cooperative venture in which the federal government and relevant states participate as equals. The commission is composed of the governors (or their representatives) of the 13 states and a federal co-chairman appointed by the president. The regional, state and local development district levels each have their own responsibilities. At the regional level ARC attempts to assess Appalachia's future role in the national economy and is concerned with developing regional programs, planning for public facilities, cooperating in interstate programs, and undertaking social and economic analyses. The role of state planning is to determine areas with significant potential for future growth, formulate long run programs and annual project plans geared to each Appalachian subarea in the state and establish local development districts within which federal, state and local planning efforts are to be coordinated. The multicounty development districts are responsible for communicating local needs and aspirations to the states, developing local development projects and coordinating their local execution.

Growth Centers

In contrast to the wide scattering of public investments that had characterized earlier efforts to aid depressed areas, the ARDA specified that those "made in the region under this Act shall be concentrated in areas where there is the greatest potential for future growth, and where the expected return on public dollars will be the greatest."

What degree of project concentration has actually been achieved by ARC? Probably the best indication of success in this regard is provided by the data in Table 3–1. The four level categorization shown there was developed by ARC and applied to each state plan. Level 1 was defined as the highest level of growth potential in each state. Level 4 areas were not designated as growth areas, while the other levels represent different degrees of intermediate situations. The data presented in Table 3–1 do not include projects that were made before growth areas were defined and they do not include certain outlays that could not be localized. For all of Appalachia, 62 percent of investment funds went to the dominant growth

Table 3-1. Concentration of Appalachian Program Investments in Growth Areas, by State, 1965-1970

| State | Growth Area Levels | | | |
	1 (Percent)	2 (Percent)	3 (Percent)	4 (Percent)
Alabama	84.3	1.4	—	14.3
Georgia	33.2	27.1	—	39.7
Kentucky	2.2	45.8	42.0	9.9
Maryland	86.0	14.0	—	—
Mississippi	87.2	6.9	—	5.9
North Carolina	17.3	36.5	43.4	2.8
New York	80.5	9.9	—	9.6
Ohio	87.2	9.7	—	3.1
Pennsylvania	86.1	4.8	2.9	6.2
South Carolina	68.6	9.1	—	21.3
Tennessee	38.7	26.5	24.3	10.5
Virginia	61.5	—	—	38.5
West Virginia	67.3	3.0	9.5	20.2
Region	62.1	13.9	10.3	13.7

Source: Monroe Newman, *The Political Economy of Appalachia* (Lexington, Mass.: D.C. Heath and Company, 1972), p. 156.

areas of each state during the first five years of ARC's operations. Only 14 percent went to areas that were felt to have no growth potential. Kentucky's low proportion of Level 1 investments reflects the fact that it has only one Appalachian county that is part of a multistate SMSA. The relatively low Level 1 outlays in Georgia, North Carolina and Tennessee reflect state decisions to promote growth away from the largest SMSAs. Moreover, those states with the highest proportions of Level 4 investments for the most part concentrated their funds on human resource projects rather than those more directly associated with economic development.

Human Resources

The issue of investment in human resources has been a key one in the history of the Appalachian program. The original ARDA made highway development a substantial part of the program on the ground that lack of accessibility was holding back the progress of the region. Of the initial $1.1 billion authorization, $840 million was allocated to highway construction over a five year period, while another $252 million was allocated to a number of other social and economic programs for a two year period. Bringing the two types of outlays down to a two year basis and adding matching state funds meant that about $480 million was authorized for highways and approximately $281 million for 11 other major categories.

The ARDA's initial emphasis on highway construction was severely criticized in some quarters. On the other hand, there has been strong support for the highway program within ARC, primarily because it has been regarded as the matrix within which human resource investments will prove their effectiveness. Thus, Ralph Widner, the very able executive director of ARC during its first six years, could argue in reviewing the Appalachian experience that:

> the critics argued that it makes far better sense to invest in people than in the concrete of highways. Most of us would agree.
>
> But how carefully thought through is that criticism? If children cannot get to a school for lack of decent transportation, if a pregnant mother cannot get to a hospital for lack of a decent road, if a breadwinner cannot get to a job because the job 30 miles away cannot be reached in a reasonable time, then is such an investment an investment in people or an investment in concrete?[55]

Moreover, in practice there has been a complete reorientation of nonhighway funds during the life of ARC. From an original preference for physical resource investments in the ARDA, ARC has moved to a three-to-one preference for human resource projects in terms of actual project expenditures. (ARC is not authorized to undertake manpower programs, but it is common for ARC-funded vocational training facilities to be used at night for training under various manpower programs.) And this comparison understates the case because it leaves out the human resource emphasis of supplemental fund allocations. Finally, under one of the more innovative sections of the ARDA, ARC is given funds to supplement local funds in the financing of federal grant-in-aid programs so that the local contribution can be reduced to as low as 20 percent of the project's cost. Newman maintains that through August 1971, $215 million had been appropriated for supplemental funds; almost 82 percent of this total was spent on human resource development.

The reasoning behind the shift in emphasis toward human resource investments has been stated by him in the following terms:

> By investing heavily in the most mobile form of resources—people—the commission was able to minimize the chance that its investments would be wasted. Though no one could be sure that any particular set of public facility investments could contribute to the development of a self-supporting economy in the more lagging portions of the region, it was clear that better health and education for the people of those areas was a necessary precondition for such development if it was to occur, and, if it did not, individuals could carry them wherever opportunities were available.[56]

This approach would seem to be a milestone on the road from place-oriented policies toward approaches recognizing that the welfare of people is, or should be, the principal objective of economic policy.

NOTES

[1] Ray Marshall, *Rural Workers in Rural Labor Markets* (Salt Lake City: Olympus Publishing Co., 1974), pp. 89–90.

[2] François Perroux, "Note sur la notion de pôle de croissance," *Economie Appliquée* (janvier-juin 1955), pp. 307–20; Albert O. Hirschman, *The Strategy of Economic Development* (New Haven: Yale University Press, 1958); Gunnar Myrdal, *Rich Lands and Poor* (New York: Harper and Brothers, 1957).

[3] Niles M. Hansen, *French Regional Planning* (Bloomington, Ind.: Indiana University Press; and Edinburgh: Edinburgh University Press, 1968), pp. 119–20.

[4] See, for example J.R. Lasuén, "On Growth Poles," *Urban Studies* 6, 2 (May 1969): 137–61, reprinted in Niles M. Hansen, *Growth Centers in Regional Economic Development* (New York: The Free Press, 1972), pp. 20–49; Malcolm J. Moseley "Growth Centres—A Shibboleth?" *Area* 5, 2 (1973): 143–50; and D. Todd, "An Appraisal of the Development Pole Concept in Regional Analysis," *Environment and Planning* 6, 3 (May-June 1974): 291–306; C.W. Moore, "Industrial Linkage Development Paths in Growth Poles: A Research Methodology," *Environment and Planning* 4, 3 (March-April 1972): 253–71.

It may be noted that growth center theory has now entered the field of vision of the "radical geographers." For several prime examples of rediscovering the wheel, see *Antipode: A Radical Journal of Geography* 6, 2 (July 1974).

[5] George A. Collier, Jr., "On the Size and Spacing of Growth Centers: Comment," *Growth and Change* 4, 4 (October 1973): 47.

[6] William Alonso and Elliott Medrich, "Spontaneous Growth Centers in Twentieth-Century American Urbanization," in Niles M. Hansen, *Growth Centers in Regional Economic Development* (New York: The Free Press, 1972), p. 230.

[7] Lloyd Rodwin, *Nations and Cities* (Boston: Houghton Mifflin, 1970), p. 8.

[8] John B. Parr, "Growth Poles, Regional Development, and Central Place Theory," *Papers of the Regional Science Association* 31 (1973): 175. See also Emilio Casetti, Leslie King and John Odlund, "The Formalization and Testing of Concepts of Growth Poles in a Spatial Context," *Environment and Planning* 3, 4 (1971): 377–82; and G. Robinson and K. Salih, "The Spread of Development Around Kuala Lumpur: A Methodology for an Exploratory Test of Some Assumptions of the Growth Pole Model," *Regional Studies* 5 (1971): 303–14.

[9] While it is true that Perroux's initial paper on growth poles neglected the spatial dimension and was not directly concerned with policy matters, the output of the French school almost immediately became oriented to policy issues in a spatial context. The original work of Hirschman and Myrdal was clearly concerned from the start with regional policy. Thus, I do not hesitate to use the terms "growth pole" (which to some writers implies intersectoral relations abstracted from space) and "growth center" as equivalent expressions implying regional policy concerns.

[10] Collier.

[11] Niles M. Hansen, *Intermediate-Size Cities as Growth Centers* (New York: Praeger, 1971).

[12] Alonso and Medrich.

[13] Another difficulty is that "[i]f homogeneous regions are good candidates for input-output models, strongly nodal regions may be poor candidates unless the

boundaries of the region conform closely to the outer limits of the gravitational field of influence of the dominant node, and even then an important condition must be that this 'force field' should not overlap with that of a node outside the region." Harry W. Richardson, *Input-Output and Regional Economics* (New York: John Wiley and Sons, 1972), p. 87.

[14] Brian J.L. Berry, "City Size Distributions and Economic Development," *Economic Development and Cultural Change* 9, 4, p. 1 (July 1961): 587.

[15] Edwin von Böventer, "City Size Systems: Theoretical Issues, Empirical Regularities, and Planning Guides," *Urban Studies* 10, 2 (June 1973): 145–62.

[16] Parr, p. 202.

[17] Ibid.

[18] Brian J.L. Berry, *Growth Centers in the American Urban System*, vol. 1 (Cambridge, Mass.: Ballinger, 1973), p. 8.

[19] Ibid., p. 9.

[20] Brian J.L. Berry, "Hierarchical Diffusion: The Basis of Developmental Filtering and Spread in a System of Growth Centers," in Niles M. Hansen, *Growth Centers in Regional Economic Development* (New York: The Free Press, 1972), p. 108.

[21] Berry, *Growth Centers*, p. 8. See also Berry, "Hierarchical Diffusion," pp. 114–17.

[22] See Niles M. Hansen, *The Challenge of Urban Growth: The Basic Economics of City Size and Structure* (Lexington, Mass.: D.C. Heath, 1975), ch. 5.

[23] Allan R. Pred, "The Growth and Development of Systems of Cities in Advanced Economies," in *Systems of Cities and Information Flows* (Lund, Sweden: Lund Studies in Geography, Series B, No. 38, 1973), p. 36.

[24] Berry, "Hierarchical Diffusion," pp. 118–34.

[25] Berry, *Growth Centers*, pp. 55–115.

[26] Parr, p. 202.

[27] See Everett M. Rogers, with F. Floyd Shoemaker, *Communication of Innovations*, 2nd ed. (New York: The Free Press, 1971). Although this study does not give much emphasis to the spatial transmission of innovations, it clearly illustrates the complexity and ambiguity of innovation diffusion processes.

[28] Todd, p. 303.

[29] Economic Development Administration, *Program Evaluation: The Economic Development Administration Growth Center Strategy* (Washington, D.C.: EDA, 1972), p. 5.

[30] Brian J.L. Berry, "Spatial Organization and Levels of Welfare: Degree of Metropolitan Labor Market Participation as a Variable in Economic Development" (Paper presented to the Economic Development Administration Research Conference, Washington, D.C., October 9–13, 1967), p. 12.

[31] *Report to the Congress on the Proposal for an Economic Adjustment Program* (Washington, D.C.: Department of Commerce and the Office of Management and Budget, February, 1974), p. 10.

[32] Ibid., p. 25.

[33] Dominick Salvatore, "The Operation of the Market Mechanism and Regional Inequality," *Kyklos* 25, 3 (1972): 518–36.

[34] William B. Beyers, "Growth Centers and Interindustry Linkages" (Unpub-

lished paper, Department of Geography, University of Washington, Seattle). See also Rodney A. Erickson, "The Regional Impact of Growth Firms: The Case of Boeing, 1963–1968," *Land Economics* 50, 2 (May 1974): 127–36.

[35] Gary L. Gaile, "Growth Center Theory: An Analysis of Its Formal Spatial-Temporal Aspects" (Paper presented at the Southern California Academy of Sciences Annual Meeting, Long Beach, May 5, 1973), p. 12.

[36] Gary L. Gaile, "Notes on the Concept of 'Spread' " (Unpublished paper, Department of Geography, UCLA, 1973), p. 15.

[37] Irwin Gray, "Employment Effect of a New Industry in a Rural Area," *Monthly Labor Review* 92, 6 (June 1969): p. 29. For a comparable Flemish example, see Olivier Vanneste, *The Growth Pole Concept and the Regional Economic Policy* (Bruges: De Tempel, 1971), pp. 78–79.

[38] Vida Nichols, "Growth Poles: An Evaluation of Their Propulsive Effect," *Environment and Planning* 1, 2 (1969): 199.

[39] M.J. Moseley, "The Impact of Growth Centres in Rural Regions," *Regional Studies* 7, 1 (March 1973): 93.

[40] See Berry, *Growth Centers,* vol. 2; and Niles M. Hansen, *The Future of Nonmetropolitan America* (Lexington, Mass.: D.C. Heath, 1973).

[41] The case for smaller growth centers in lagging areas is relatively well stated in Richard L. Morrill, "On the Size and Spacing of Growth Centers," *Growth and Change* 4, 2 (April 1973): 21–24. However, a more persuasive contrary argument is given in Richard Lamb and Quentin Gillard, "Growth Center Schemes Evaluated," in Brian J.L. Berry, *Growth Centers in the American Urban System*, vol. 1 (Cambridge, Mass.: Ballinger, 1973), pp. 165–87.

[42] Niles M. Hansen, *Location Preferences, Migration, and Regional Growth* (New York: Praeger, 1973).

[43] See Hansen, *Future of Nonmetropolitan America;* and Richard F. Lamb, "Metropolitan Impacts on Rural America" (Dissertation to be published in 1975 as a monograph (no. 162) in the University of Chicago Department of Geography research series).

[44] Vanneste, pp. 250–58.

[45] Morgan D. Thomas, "Growth Pole Theory: An Examination of Some of Its Basic Concepts," in Niles M. Hansen, *Growth Centers in Regional Economic Development* (New York: The Free Press, 1972), pp. 50–81; and "Growth Pole Theory, Technological Change and Regional Economic Growth," *Papers of the Regional Science Association* 33 (1975), forthcoming.

[46] At this writing the project has resulted in 27 published papers and seven dissertations. Hopefully an effort will be made to synthesize the project's findings.

[47] J.R. Lasuén, "Urbanisation and Development—The Temporal Interaction between Geographical and Sectoral Clusters," *Urban Studies* 10, 2 (June 1973): p. 163.

[48] Ibid., p. 164.

[49] J.R. Lasuén, "An Open System Model of Multiregional Economic Development" (Unpublished paper, Antonomous University of Madrid, September 1971).

[50] Lasuén, "Urbanisation and Development," p. 186.

[51] Ibid.

[52] Pred, p. 60.

[53] Ibid., p. 62.

[54] J.B. Goddard, "Organizational Information Flows and the Urban System" (Paper presented at the Conference on National Settlement Systems and Strategies, International Institute for Applied Systems Analysis, Laxenburg, Austria, December 16–19, 1974). See also Gunnar Törnqvist, "Swedish Industry as a Spatial System, (Paper presented at the Conference on National Settlement Systems and Strategies, International Institute for Applied Systems Analysis, Laxenburg, Austria, December 16–19, 1974); and his "Contact Requirement and Travel Facilities," in *Systems of Cities and Information Flows* (Lund, Sweden: Lund Studies in Geography, Series B, No. 38, 1973).

[55] Ralph Widner, "Appalachia After Six Years," *Appalachia* 5, 6 (1971): 19.

[56] Monroe Newman, *The Political Economy of Appalachia* (Lexington, Mass.: D.C. Heath and Company, 1972), p. 150.

Chapter Four

Delineating Nonmetropolitan Planning Regions

It has been widely recognized for some time that the individual rural county is not in itself a viable economic planning unit. In recent years the states, under pressure from the federal government, have been delineating multi-county planning districts, but no attempt has been made to apply uniform criteria in this regard. Meanwhile, university scholars and federal government professional staff members—often working in concert—have sought to delineate nationally exhaustive functional economic areas. Although there have been differences in approach, the criteria in each case have been applied consistently to the nation as a whole. The rationale behind each of the major national delineations is examined critically in this chapter; the perspective adopted is that of the efficient organization of nonmetropolitan labor markets. Nonmetropolitan planning mechanisms as they exist within the context of state-designated multicounty planning units are evaluated in the chapter which follows.

ECONOMIC SPACE

From an economic point of view there are three types of space: homogeneous, polarized and program—or planning—space. Thus, in the first place,

> [t]he region can be characterized by its more or less pronounced uniformity: it is more or less homogeneous. In the second place, the region can be studied from the point of view of its more or less pronounced degree of coherence, that is to say, according to the interdependence of its diverse parts; it is more or less polarized. Finally, the region can be envisaged from the point of view of the goal that is pursues, of the program that it establishes; this is the program region or planning region.[1]

In this approach a *homogeneous* region corresponds to a continuous space wherein each of the constituent parts or zones has relevant characteristics as close as possible to those of the others. In contrast, the notion of *polarized* space is closely related to that of a hierarchy of urban centers ranked according to the functions they perform; a polarized region is a heterogeneous space whose different parts complement and support one another, and where these parts have more exchanges of goods and services with a dominant intraregional urban center, or pole, than with neighboring regions. Moreover, there are three types of polarization: national, regional and local. This hierarchy corresponds to the hierarchy of specialized goods and services which are produced or furnished at these levels. Thus, national goods circulate throughout a given country, regional goods are characterized by a distribution network for the most part limited to the boundaries of a given region and local goods are generally provided for only a small local market. A national center would therefore also be a regional and local center; it would perform the whole range of polarized functions. Finally, the *planning* region "is a space whose various parts depend on the same decision"; it is, in addition, "an instrument placed in the hands of an authority, whether or not localized in the region, to attain a given economic goal."[2] While there exist as many program regions as there are distinct problems, the interdependence of diverse activities requires a program region chosen with the intention of coordinating solutions to various problems.

Regional delineations of the United States have been made within the context of each of these major orientations; the major ones will now be considered in turn.

PRINCIPAL DELINEATIONS

Bureau of Economic Analysis Regions

The Regional Economics Division of BEA (formerly known as the Office of Business Economics, or OBE), U.S. Department of Commerce, carries out a continuing program of regional measurement, analysis and projection of economic activity. To facilitate this program BEA has defined economic areas on the basis of the polarized or, as it is sometimes called, nodal-functional concept. But whereas Boudeville's approach in this regard emphasizes flows of goods and services, the BEA approach is primarily based on commuting patterns—i.e., on functional labor market areas. These areas are essentially derived from Brian Berry's studies of Daily Urban Systems, a term coined in 1967 by C.A. Doxiadis. Doxiadis argued that "sixty DUSs were now being formed in the United States, each with an average radius of ninety miles 'within which people will move the way they now move within well-organized metropolitan areas.' "[3] Berry, however, based his analysis on the actual evidence from the 1960 census about commuting patterns around existing economic centers.

Thus, in the BEA approach surrounding county units are attached to each urban center, where economic activities are directly or indirectly focused. Insofar as possible, each BEA area combines the place of work and place of residence of employees. There is therefore a minimum of commuting across BEA area boundaries. Each area approaches self-sufficiency in its residentiary industry. That is, even though each area produces goods and services for export, most of the services and some of the goods required by the residents and firms of the area are provided within the area.

The BEA areas correspond fairly closely to the closed trade areas of central place theory, in which the number and type of firms and their size and trade areas are bounded by the relative transportation costs from hinterland to competing centers. Each area approaches closure with respect to residentiary industries that include general and convenience retail and wholesale trade activities and those other services which, because they are difficult to transport, are most efficiently consumed in the vicinity of their production. On the other hand, the areas remain largely open to the movement of transportable commodities and to nontransportable special services, such as education at Cambridge and recreation at Miami.

On the basis of his early pioneering work on functional economic area delineation, Karl Fox wrote that "[w]ith the possible exception of influence upon national farm policies, it appears to us that economic linkages and communications between the nationally-oriented center and the smaller urban places in Iowa tend to be mediated and transmitted through the cities of 25,000 population or larger which are the central cities of functional economic areas."[4] In the BEA delineation process Standard Metropolitan Statistical Areas were chosen where possible as economic centers because of their obvious significance as wholesale and retail trade centers and as labor market centers. However, not all SMSAs were made centers because some are part of larger metropolitan complexes, as in the New York area. In rural parts of the country where there are no SMSAs, cities in the 25,000 to 50,000 population range were chosen as centers, provided that two criteria were met: first, the city had to be a wholesale trade center for the area, and second, the area as a whole had to have a minimum population of about 200,000 persons, although some exceptions were made in sparsely populated areas. Once centers were identified, intervening counties were allocated to them on the basis of comparative time and distance of travel to them, the interconnection between counties because of journey to work, the road network, and other linkages and geographic features. In cases where commuting patterns overlapped, counties were included in the economic areas containing the center with which there was the greatest commuting connection. In more rural parts of the country, where journey to work information was insufficient, distance of travel to the economic centers was the major factor in establishing the boundaries of economic areas. The 173 BEA areas are shown on Map 4–1.

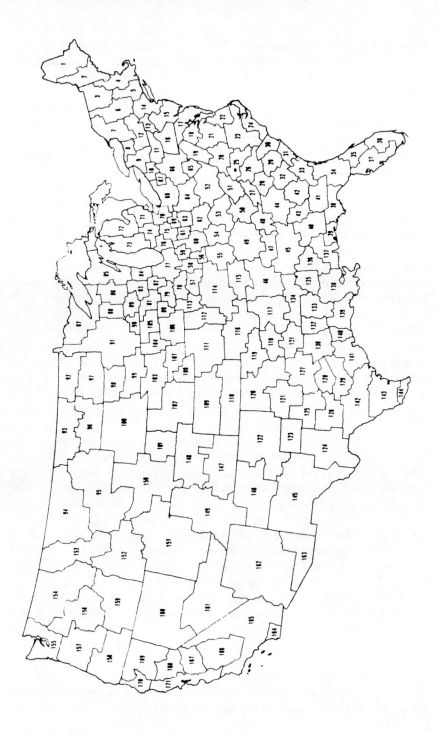

141. Houston, Tex.
142. San Antonio, Tex.
143. Corpus Christi, Tex.
144. Brownsville-Harlingen-San Benito, Tex.
145. El Paso, Tex.
146. Albuquerque, N.M.
147. Pueblo, Colo.
148. Denver, Colo.
149. Grand Junction, Colo.
150. Cheyenne, Wyo.
151. Salt Lake City, Utah
152. Idaho Falls, Idaho
153. Butte, Mont.
154. Spokane, Wash.
155. Seattle-Everett, Wash.
156. Yakima, Wash.
157. Portland, Ore.-Wash.
158. Eugene, Ore.
159. Boise City, Idaho
160. Reno, Nev.
161. Las Vegas, Nev.
162. Phoenix, Ariz.
163. Tucson, Ariz.
164. San Diego, Calif.
165. Los Angeles-Long Beach, Calif.
166. Fresno, Calif.
167. Stockton, Calif.
168. Sacramento, Calif.
169. Redding, Calif.
170. Eureka, Calif.
171. San Francisco-Oakland, Calif.
172. Anchorage, Alaska
173. Honolulu, Hawaii

106. Des Moines, Iowa
107. Omaha, Nebr.-Iowa
108. Lincoln, Nebr.
109. Salina, Kans.
110. Wichita, Kans.
111. Kansas City, Mo.-Kans.
112. Columbia, Mo.
113. Quincy, Ill.
114. St. Louis, Mo.-Ill.
115. Paducah, Ky.
116. Springfield, Mo.
117. Little Rock-No. Little Rock, Ark.
118. Fort Smith, Ark.-Okla.
119. Tulsa, Okla.
120. Oklahoma City, Okla.
121. Wichita Falls, Tex.
122. Amarillo, Tex.
123. Lubbock, Tex.
124. Odessa, Tex.
125. Abilene, Tex.
126. San Angelo, Tex.
127. Dallas, Tex.
128. Waco, Tex.
129. Austin, Tex.
130. Tyler, Tex.
131. Texarkana, Tex.-Ark.
132. Shreveport, La.
133. Monroe, La.
134. Greenville, Miss.
135. Jackson, Miss.
136. Meridian, Miss.
137. Mobile, Ala.
138. New Orleans, La.
139. Lake Charles, La.
140. Beaumont-Port Arthur-Orange, Tex.

71. Detroit, Mich.
72. Saginaw, Mich.
73. Grand Rapids, Mich.
74. Lansing, Mich.
75. Fort Wayne, Ind.
76. South Bend, Ind.
77. Chicago, Ill.
78. Peoria, Ill.
79. Davenport-Rock Island-Moline, Iowa-Ill.
80. Cedar Rapids, Iowa
81. Dubuque, Iowa
82. Rockford, Ill.
83. Madison, Wis.
84. Milwaukee, Wis.
85. Green Bay, Wis.
86. Wausau, Wis.
87. Duluth-Superior, Minn.-Wis.
88. Eau Claire, Wis.
89. La Crosse, Wis.
90. Rochester, Minn.
91. Minneapolis-St. Paul, Minn.
92. Grand Forks, N.D.
93. Minot, N.D.
94. Great Falls, Mont.
95. Billings, Mont.
96. Bismark, N.D.
97. Fargo-Moorhead, N.D.-Minn.
98. Aberdeen, S.D.
99. Sioux Falls, S.D.
100. Rapid City, S.D.
101. Scotts Bluff, Nebr.
102. Grand Island, Nebr.
103. Sioux City, Iowa-Nebr.
104. Ford Dodge, Iowa
105. Waterloo, Iowa

1. Bangor, Maine
2. Portland, Maine
3. Burlington, Vt.
4. Boston, Mass.
5. Hartford, Conn.
6. Albany-Schenectady-Troy, N.Y.
7. Syracuse, N.Y.
8. Rochester, N.Y.
9. Buffalo, N.Y.
10. Erie, Pa.
11. Williamsport, Pa.
12. Binghamton, N.Y.-Pa.
13. Wilkes-Barre-Hazelton, Pa.
14. New York, N.Y.
15. Philadelphia, Pa.-N.J.
16. Harrisburg, Pa.
17. Baltimore, Md.
18. Washington, D.C.-Md.-Va.
19. Staunton, Va.
20. Roanoke, Va.
21. Richmond, Va.
22. Norfolk-Portsmouth, Va.
23. Raleigh, N.C.
24. Wilmington, N.C.
25. Greensboro-Winston Salem-High Point, N.C.
26. Charlotte, N.C.
27. Asheville, N.C.
28. Greenville, S.C.
29. Columbia, S.C.
30. Florence, S.C.
31. Charleston, S.C.
32. Augusta, Ga.
33. Savannah, Ga.
34. Jacksonville, Fla.
35. Orlando, Fla.
36. Miami, Fla.
37. Tampa-St. Petersburg, Fla.
38. Tallahassee, Fla.
39. Pensacola, Fla.
40. Montgomery, Ala.
41. Albany, Ga.
42. Macon, Ga.
43. Columbia, Ga.-Ala.
44. Atlanta, Ga.
45. Birmingham, Ala.
46. Memphis, Tenn.-Ark.
47. Huntville, Ala.
48. Chattanooga, Tenn.-Ga.
49. Nashville, Tenn.
50. Knoxville, Tenn.
51. Bristol, Va.-Tenn.
52. Huntington-Ashland, W. Va.-Ky.-Ohio
53. Lexington, Ky.
54. Louisville, Ky.-Ind.
55. Evansville, Ind.
56. Terre Haute, Ind.
57. Springfield, Ill.
58. Champaign-Urbana, Ill.
59. Lafayette-West Lafayette, Ind.
60. Indianapolis, Ind.
61. Muncie, Ind.
62. Cincinnati, Ohio-Ky.-Ind.
63. Dayton, Ohio
64. Columbus, Ohio
65. Clarksburg, W. Va.
66. Pittsburgh, Pa.
67. Youngstown-Warren, Ohio
68. Cleveland, Ohio
69. Lima, Ohio
70. Toledo, Ohio

Source: Reprinted with permission from Brian J. L. Berry, *Growth Centers in the American Urban System,* vol. 1 (Cambridge, Mass.: Ballinger Publishing Company, 1973), p. 16. Copyright © 1973 Ballinger Publishing Company.

Map 4–1. The BEA Economic Areas.

Urban Spheres of Influence

In a 1973 study, David Huff attempted to delineate the spheres of influence of all major American cities.[5] These cities, together with their respective hinterlands, comprise an exhaustive national set of regions. A distinctive feature of this undertaking is that a model and a computer program were used in making the delineations, as opposed to subjective or empirical approaches. Consequently, the same basis was utilized in estimating the spheres of influence of all cities concerned. Moreover, the procedure is completely replicative, and delineations can be made quickly and inexpensively—desirable features if periodic monitoring is expected.

Huff employs a gravity model in which the probability of a person located at a point i traveling to an urban place j is directly related to the size of the urban place, but inversely related to the distance from i to j. The area comprising the sphere of influence of an urban place consists of a series of attraction gradients, which are isoprobability lines ranging from a probability value of less than one to a value greater than zero. The intersection of like probability contours between each pair of urban places produces a locus of points. Such lines are curves upon which an individual is indifferent between two urban places.

Past studies have used different measures to reflect the size of urban places, depending on the type of spatial interaction under consideration—e.g., population, employment, retail and wholesale sales, commodity output, etc. In Huff's analysis a measure of functional city size was sought that would encompass a number of different variables associated with city influence. Population, public services provided, retail goods and services offered, and similar variables could be combined to reflect a composite measure of city functional size. Such a measure was derived by Berry[6] in a previous factor analysis approach to the latent structure of the American urban system. Berry identified 14 such dimensions, accounting for 77 percent of the original variance of the 97 variables he used. One dimension, termed "functional size of cities in an urban hierarchy," reflects the aggregate economic power, or, more generally, the status of each city within the nation's urban hierarchy. Twenty-one of the 97 variables comprised this latent dimension. The factor scores measuring each city's rating on the functional size dimension were used for the size variable in Huff's gravity model. Those cities that had factor scores greater than 2.00 were regarded as first-order urban places. There were 73 urban places in this category. Those cities that had factor scores ranging from 0.25 to 1.99 were designated as second-order urban places, of which there were 274. The 347 cities comprising these first two levels in the urban hierarchy were used in calculating the lines of equilibrium between all pairs of cities. The boundaries of urban spheres of influence that resulted from the computer program output were altered to conform to county boundaries, since the county represents the basic geographical unit for reporting economic and social data. The following criteria were established for deriving multicounty delineations: (1) a county was assigned to the urban place whose sphere of influence encompassed the largest proportion of the county's total area; (2) if the sphere of influence of an urban place encompassed less than the major portion of a county it was eliminated; and (3) if two urban places were located in the same county the smaller of the two places was eliminated. One of the 73 first-order places and 55 of the 347 first-order and second-order places did not meet the criteria for inclusion.

Map 4–2 and Map 4–3 show, respectively, the multicounty delineations for the 72 first-order urban spheres of influence and the 292 first-order and second-order urban spheres of influence.

Basic Economic Research Areas

BERAs have been used as geographic units of analysis in a number of studies, but principally by the Economic Research Service of the U.S. Department of Agriculture. Like the delineations discussed previously, BERAs are based on the nodal-functional concept. Every county in the nation is placed in one of 482 regions according to criteria which reflect economic interdependence. These criteria involve a combination of considerations of population size of urban centers, commuting time to urban centers and trading patterns as indicated by Rand McNally. Each county is supposed to exhibit greater economic interdependence with the urban center and other counties in its own BERA than with any other urban center or counties assigned to other regions.

The BERA delineation utilized basic commuting information provided by Brian Berry's study of commuting patterns as indicated by the 1960 census survey of journey to work patterns. For each of over 300 cities, Berry determined the area within which 50 percent or more of the working residents commuted to the central city, the area within which at least 5 percent similarly commuted and the area within which some but less than 5 percent of the residents commuted. In delineating the BERAs, no 50 percent commuting areas were split off from their corresponding urban centers and as far as possible the 5 percent labor shed of an urban area was assigned to the region. Consideration also was given to geographic or topological factors affecting the nature of the relationship between a county and a nearby urban center, as well as to the condition and location of roads linking counties and urban centers.

In the BERA delineation an urban center is defined as a city which, with its adjacent suburbs, has a minimum population of 25,000. A county that contained one or more urban centers but was also strongly interrelated with a more dominant urban center in another county was assigned to the region corresponding to the dominant urban center. However, most of the popula-

Map 4–2.   Multicounty Delineations of 72 Urban Spheres of Influence.

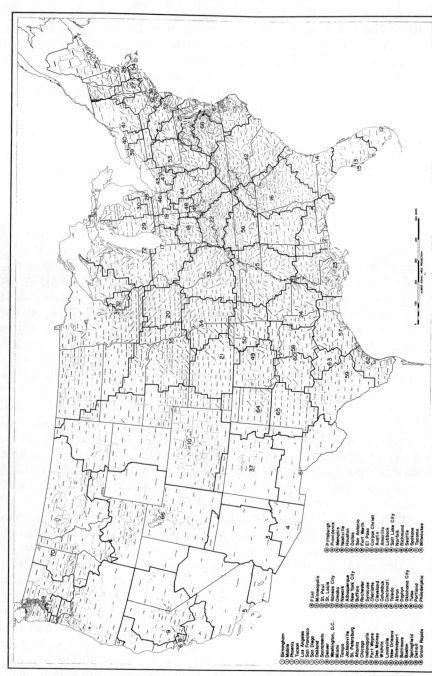

Source: Prepared by David L. Huff, University of Texas of Austin, November, 1971, for the
Office of Economic Opportunity under Grant CG 6611 A/O (Planning for Growth
and Development in Rural Areas in the Context of a National System of Regions).
Cartographer: Alice Lo.

tion of that county must be within two hours commuting time of the core urban center. If the county had no urban center but was economically interdependent with an urban center within two hours commuting time from most of its residents, then the county was assigned to the region corresponding to the urban center. If the county had no urban center and was not within two hours commuting time of an urban center, it was grouped with similar neighboring counties; thus, such regions were formed around cities with less than 25,000 population. In other words, the criterion concerning size of urban place was sacrificed in favor of the commuting criterion. Although commuting from neighboring counties to the small urban center was negligible, it was felt that it could take place if the center were to develop employment opportunities and quality services. (At the other extreme, where commuting fields of several urban centers over-lapped in high population density areas, counties were assigned to the region with which their economic interdependence was the greatest.) No criterion was established with respect to a minimal region population size or with respect to a minimum number of counties.

State Economic Areas

In contrast to the basically nodal-functional delineations that have been considered thus far, SEAs represent relatively homogeneous subdivisions of states. They consist of counties or groups of counties which have similar economic and social characteristics. SEAs were originally delineated for the 1950 census as a product of a special study sponsored by the Bureau of the Census in cooperation with the Bureau of Agricultural Economics and several state and private agencies. The delineation process was devised by Donald Bogue, then of the Scripps Foundation, on loan to the Bureau of the Census. Originally 501 SEAs were identified, but in the interest of increasing the stability of sample data some sparsely settled adjacent areas were combined, reducing the number of areas for which data were reported to 453. At the time of the 1960 census no attempt was made to reexamine the original principles or to apply them to more recent data relating to homogeneity. However, modifications made in recognition of changes in the composition of certain SMSAs, and the inclusion of Alaska and Hawaii, increased the number of SEAs to 509. With the exception of one SEA added in Wisconsin, the areas for which 1970 census data are reported are the same as those used in 1960.

In delineating SEAs, three sources of information and data were used: (1) previous descriptions of areas and previous area delineations made by geographers, economists and others interested in regional differences; (2) data about the economy and population of each county available from census material and other government reports; and (3) opinions, criticism, advice and suggestions made by specialists who resided in particular areas

Map 4–3. Multicounty Delineations of 292 Urban Spheres of Influence.

Source: Same as for map 4–2.

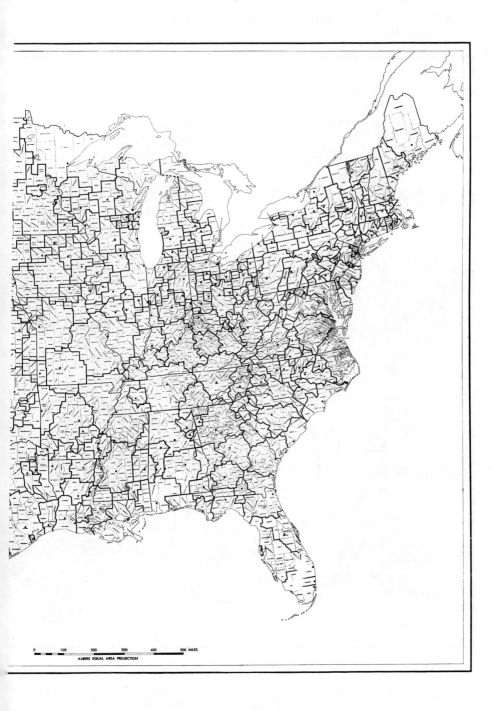

0   100   200   300   400   500 MILES

ALBERS EQUAL AREA PROJECTION

Map 4–4. Basic Economic Research Areas of the United States, October 1, 1970.

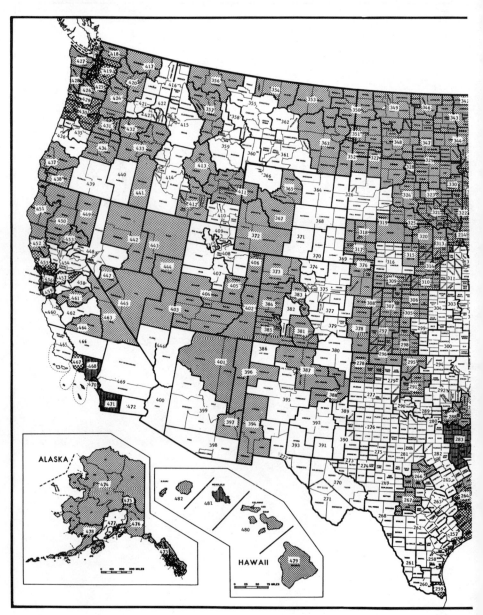

Source: Economic Research Service, NEG. ERS. 7949–71 (1).

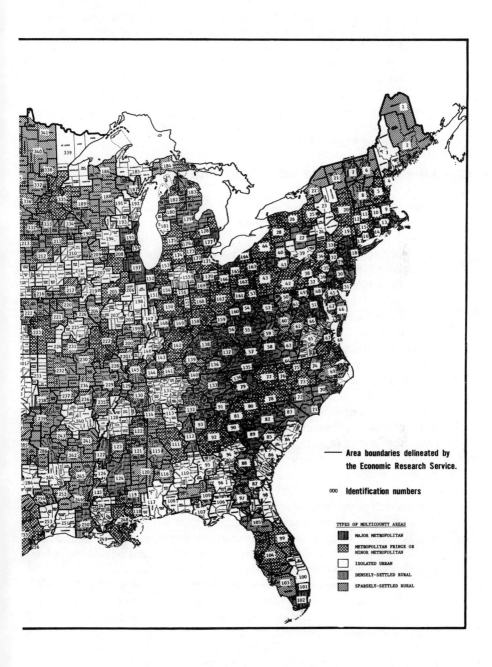

Area boundaries delineated by
the Economic Research Service.

000   Identification numbers

TYPES OF MULTICOUNTY AREAS

MAJOR METROPOLITAN

METROPOLITAN FRINGE OR
MINOR METROPOLITAN

ISOLATED URBAN

DENSELY-SETTLED RURAL

SPARSELY-SETTLED RURAL

or by persons who otherwise had first-hand familiarity with them. General impressions and informal observations were relied upon only when no other conclusive data were to be had. Homogeneity with respect to economic and social conditions was a principal criterion in judging the quality of the delineations. However, all state boundaries were regarded as SEA boundaries, a condition imposed in order to permit the publication of SEA data for each state. Despite this constraint, care was taken to make it possible to integrate SEA boundaries across state lines so that data could be summarized for a few major economic and resource areas.[7] The SEAs are shown on Map 4–5.

AN ASSESSMENT OF THE DELINEATIONS

In terms of functional labor market analysis, the BEA regions are in many respects a clear improvement over any previously delineated economic units of analysis. Clearly the county is too small. Whole states usually are too large and contain multiple labor market areas; moreover, state political boundaries often have no more economic meaning than county boundaries. The great advantage of the BEA regions is that they have been specifically delineated on the basis of the fact that the spatial economic organization of the country is closely related to its urban system.

Use of the BEA regions focuses attention on the interdependencies between nonmetropolitan counties and SMSAs, and it provides a vehicle for analyzing the welfare consequences of access to SMSAs. Nevertheless, the SMSA orientation of the BEA regions poses some problems for the analysis of rural labor markets, especially in areas where few or no workers commute to an SMSA. It will be recalled from Chapter One that Berry's interpretation of his commuting studies, which underlie the BEA delineations, tended to exaggerate the number of persons living within commuting distance of SMSAs; and that Beale found that in 1960 two-thirds of the rural population lived in counties where fewer than 5 percent of the workers commuted to an SMSA. Obviously there are many millions of Americans who cannot or will not commute or migrate to SMSAs. The labor markets that are relevant to them are much smaller than BEA regions, although, as will be shown later, there exist numerous nonmetropolitan multicounty areas where 100,000 or more people live within commuting distance of one another, but not within commuting distance to SMSAs.

In sum, then, the process by which the BEA regions were delineated is valid and useful for most labor market policy purposes. Moreover, the great majority of Americans live within BEA urban centers and their contiguous urban field hinterlands. Nevertheless, the relevance of the BEA regions to problems of more distant hinterland areas is quite limited and the total population of these areas is far from negligible.

The urban spheres of influence delineated by Huff pose different problems. The set of regions based on first-order urban places (Map 4–2) is clearly unsatisfactory in the present context because it magnifies the difficulties just discussed with regard to the BEA regions. The regionalization based on 292 first-order and second-order urban places (Map 4–3) appears to be more appropriate, but it suffers from a common problem in Huff's general approach. For one thing, it is based on a factor analysis by Berry, which in turn has been sharply criticized by Robert Alford.

> The purpose for which a classification of cities is devised should determine not only the selection of a unit of analysis and the particular set of those units but also the choice of data that are collected and summarized about those units. Berry makes the same point . . . but he fails to consider its relevance to the selection of 97 primary variables included in his factor analysis. In fact no criteria for the inclusion of those 97 primary variables are presented. The result is that the factor structure that is produced necessarily reflects the nature of the input data, which refer primarily to the characteristics of the population, labor force, economic base, income and a variety of demographic indicators.
>
> . . . .
>
> In fact it could be argued that the factor analysis prevents *any* causal inferences, because it artificially lumps some variables under one factor and others under another factor in a manner that exaggerates their independence and makes it difficult to analyze their relationships.[8]

Even more to the point, it will be recalled that Huff's model relies on factor scores representing a "latent dimension" of American cities entitled "functional size of cities in an urban hierarchy." Alford points out that "Berry finds a size factor because he includes a number of labor-force characteristics highly correlated with size, as well as the size of the city counted twice, 5 years apart. Given the arbitrariness of the selection of variables, the factor structure is determined by the selection of certain variables and not others."[9] It is therefore not surprising that an empirical study using Huff's regions found them to be unsatisfactory. This report presents the conclusions of six intensive on-site case studies of rural economic growth in the United States. Changes in the level of employment in each area were the central concern of the research, though the study was designed to provide as broad a view as possible of factors contributing to employment growth and the consequences of such growth. The six regions examined were originally selected from Huff's set of 292 regions. They included the areas surrounding Lafayette and Lake Charles, Louisiana; Springfield and Marion, Ohio; and San Angelo and Midland-Odessa, Texas. The researchers found that:

Map 4–5. Economic Subregions and State Economic Areas, 1970.

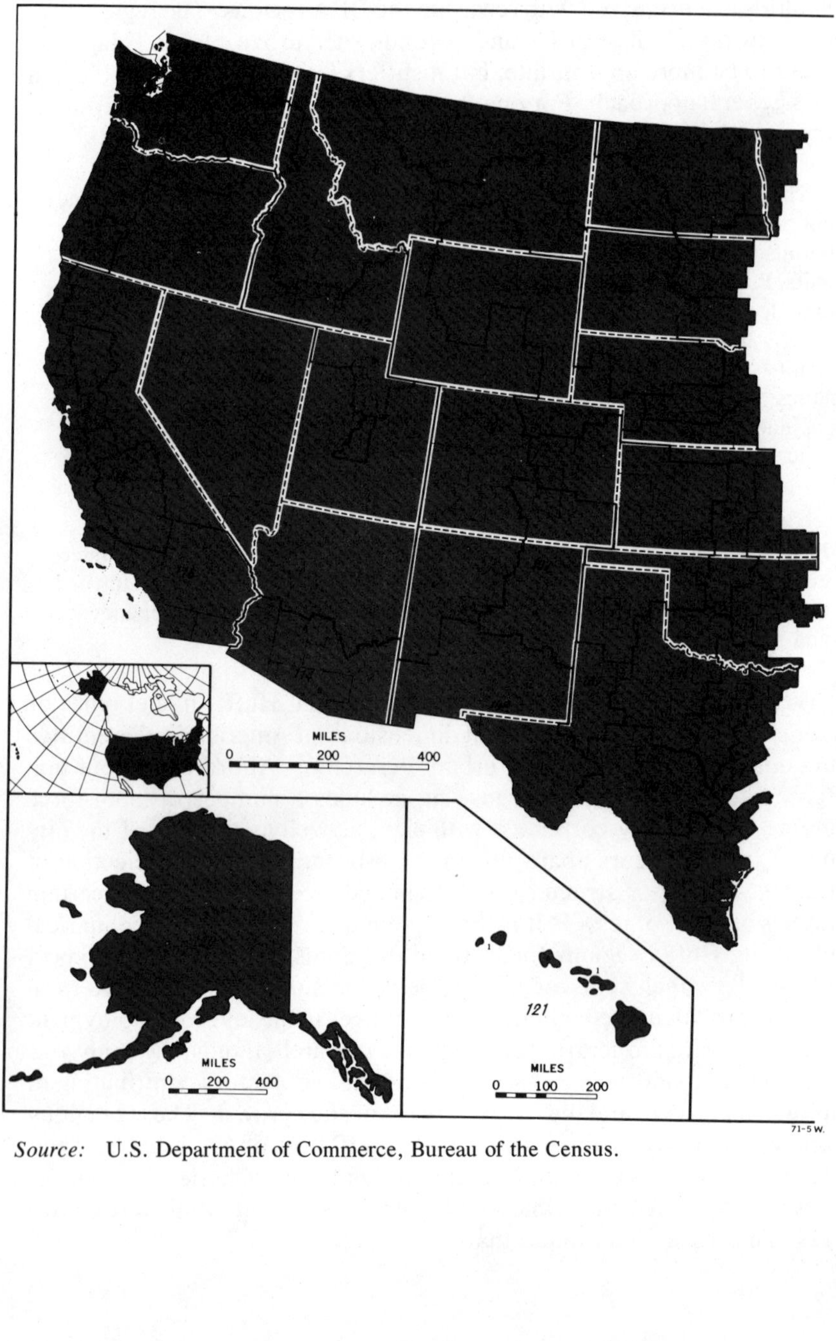

Source: U.S. Department of Commerce, Bureau of the Census.

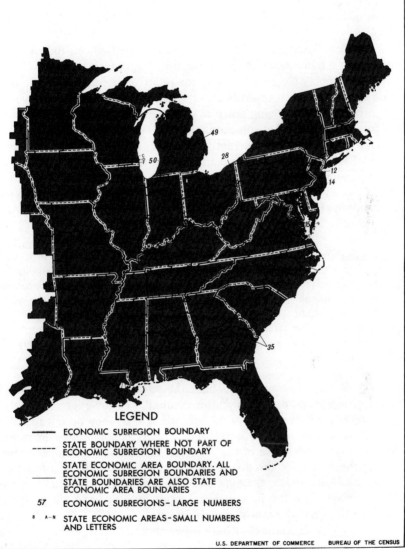

LEGEND

——— ECONOMIC SUBREGION BOUNDARY

----- STATE BOUNDARY WHERE NOT PART OF
ECONOMIC SUBREGION BOUNDARY

——— STATE ECONOMIC AREA BOUNDARY. ALL
ECONOMIC SUBREGION BOUNDARIES AND
STATE BOUNDARIES ARE ALSO STATE
ECONOMIC AREA BOUNDARIES

57   ECONOMIC SUBREGIONS – LARGE NUMBERS

8   A-N   STATE ECONOMIC AREAS – SMALL NUMBERS
AND LETTERS

U.S. DEPARTMENT OF COMMERCE   BUREAU OF THE CENSUS

71-5E.

The regional system used as a basis for the site selection in this study is an interesting application of a technique of mathematical geography. In each of the case study areas, however, the original region did not correspond to an integrated economic unit. In some cases, counties which the core cities in fact influenced were omitted and in others, counties were included that have little or no economic connection with the core city.[10]

The Basic Economic Research Areas (Map 4–4), on the other hand, represent a more realistic nodal-functional approach in hinterland areas. This is probably a consequence of the relatively nonmetropolitan orientation of the persons responsible for the delineation. The process was based on urban centers ranging down in size to 25,000 persons, but it also took account of the fact that some areas should be regarded as separate regions even though they do not currently contain a center of even this modest size. The BERAs also have the advantage that their size and location bear at least a rough correspondence to many substate planning district delineations (see Map 4–6). Indeed, it would not take much imagination to modify many of the BERAs so that they conform with district boundaries. After all it is readily admitted that frequently

> it was difficult to determine the BERA to which a particular county should belong, either because some of the criteria led to conflicting possibilities, or because none of the criteria indicated the existence of strong economic interdependencies among counties. In these ambiguous cases, the assignment of counties to BERA's was to some extent arbitrary. A different weighting of the factors could lead to other groupings of the counties involved. Counties on the borders of the BERA's are the ones most likely to be in this situation.[11]

The State Economic Areas have the advantage that census data have been grouped and published in this context. Yet however accurately they may reflect relatively homogeneous subregions, they do not readily lend themselves to development planning. The SEA boundaries are not easily reconcilable with those of the districts. Of course, one might argue "so much the worse for the districts." However, SEAs have a fundamental conceptual drawback: they are essentially descriptive and do not provide much insight into the functional relations involved in such processes as service delivery and innovation diffusion.

The results of studies by Clark Edwards and Robert Coltrane represent another reason for having reasonable confidence in the BERA and district frameworks. They compared alternative delineations of multicounty areal observation units from the point of view of analyzing rural development problems. The nine delineations used were: (1) 3,068 counties; (2) 509 substate planning areas designated by state governors; (3) 507 SEAs; (4)

Map 4–6. Substate Planning and Development Districts, March, 1974

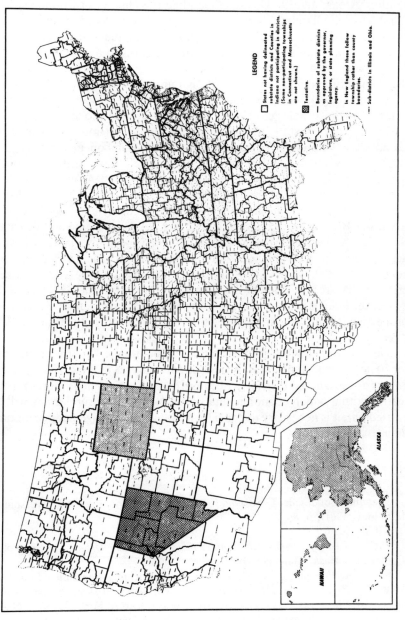

Source: U.S. Department of Agriculture, Economic Research Service, NEG. ERS. 7948–74 (3).

489 Rand McNally Basic Trading Areas; (5) 472 BERA regions; (6) 171 BEA regions; (7) 119 aggregates of SEAs; (8) 49 Rand McNally Major Trading Areas; and (9) 49 states including the District of Columbia. The Rand McNally Trading Areas have not been considered in detail in the present study because the precise uniform conceptual foundation of their delineation has not been specified. However, it is known that Rand Mc-Nally works with empirical evidence on trading area linkages rather than the commuting logic of other functional area delineations.

The nine regionalization schemes were tested by Edwards and Coltrane in terms of 12 variables covering a broad spectrum of economic and social attributes. In one test the 12 variables were aggregated into a single index of economic development by means of principal component analysis. The BERAs were chosen as the basis of comparison, and the difference between each delineation coefficient and that for the BERAs was calculated. On this basis the various regionalization schemes were virtually indistinguishable. Moreover, the absolute difference in coefficients was the lowest when the BERAs were compared with the governor-delineated districts. Statistical properties also were compared when specific variables were not aggregated. In this instance comparisons of means, variances and coefficients of skewness showed that the descriptive properties of a specific variable are a function of the delineation. However, the BERAs and the governor-delineated districts again appeared to have similar descriptive properties (as did SEAs, BEA regions and Rand McNally Basic Trading Areas).[12]

The authors conclude that the apparent economic structure estimated for BERAs could appropriately be used for analyses of relationships in the governor-designated districts. Because these districts now represent the matrix within which economic and social planning for rural areas will be carried out, it is necessary to consider their nature and significance in some detail.

NOTES

[1] Jacques Boudeville, *Les espaces économiques* (Paris: Presses Universitaires de France, 1961), p. 8.

[2] Ibid., p. 16.

[3] Brian J.L. Berry, *Growth Centers in the American Urban System*, vol. 1 (Cambridge, Mass.: Ballinger, 1973), p. 11.

[4] Karl A. Fox and T. Krishna Kumar, "Delineating Functional Economic Areas," in *Research and Education for Regional and Area Development* (Ames: Iowa State University Press, 1966), p. 344. See also Karl A. Fox, "Metamorphosis in America: A New Synthesis of Rural and Urban Society," in William Gore and Leroy Hodapp, eds., *Change in the Small Community* (New York: Friendship Press, 1967), pp. 62–104.

⁵ David L. Huff, "The Delineation of a National System of Planning Regions on the Basis of Urban Spheres of Influence," *Regional Studies* 7 (1973): 323–29.

⁶ Brian J.L. Berry, ed., *City Classification Handbook* (New York: John Wiley and Sons, 1972).

⁷ For detailed discussion of the procedure by which the SEAs were delimited, see Donald J. Bogue and Calvin L. Beale, *Economic Areas of the United States* (Glencoe, Ill.: The Free Press, 1961), pp. 1142–56.

⁸ Robert R. Alford, "Critical Evaluation of the Principles of City Classification," in Brian J.L. Berry, ed., *City Classification Handbook* (New York: John Wiley and Sons, 1972), p. 333.

⁹ Ibid., pp. 333–34.

¹⁰ *Employment Growth in Rural Areas: Case Studies and Analysis of Regional Development* (Cambridge, Mass.: Urban Systems Research and Engineering, Inc., 1973), p. 29.

¹¹ Karen M. Nelson and Fred H. Abel, "Basic Economic Research Areas: A Delineation and Prospects for Use" (Unpublished paper, November 1971), p. 7. This paper is available from the Economic Research Service, U.S. Department of Agriculture.

¹² Clark Edwards and Robert Coltrane, "Areal Delineations for Rural Economic Development Research," *Agricultural Economics Research* 24, 3 (July 1972): 67–76; and "Economic and Social Indicators of Rural Development from an Economic Viewpoint," *Southern Journal of Agricultural Economics* (July 1972), pp. 229–45.

Chapter Five

Substate Regional Planning and the A–95 Review Process

LACK OF COORDINATION IN THE FEDERAL SYSTEM

As interest in regional development and planning grew during the 1960s, so did the number of federal and state agencies providing aid and assistance to multijurisdictional areas. However, each agency determined its own criteria for regional delineations; these delineations were uncoordinated with each other and often conflicted with the boundaries of state-designated multicounty planning areas. Moreover, each agency developed its own procedures for selecting members of local governing boards which determined project priorities and each had its own reporting system. Uncertainty about the amount, purpose and timing of financial assistance requested by various groups within their borders caused the states to view federal funds as supplementary to the planning process, rather than an integral part of it. In 1966, President Johnson issued a memorandum urging the prevention of conflict and duplication among federally assisted comprehensive planning efforts. He further requested that federally assisted planning and development districts be consistent with state planning regions and directed relevant agencies to work with the Bureau of the Budget toward these goals. In response, BOB Circular A–80 was issued in January 1967. Its main provisions were incorporated into BOB Circular A–95, "Evaluation, Review, and Coordination of Federal and Federally Assisted Programs and Projects," issued on July 24, 1969.

THE A–95 REVIEW PROCESS

The heart of A–95 is found in the Project Notification and Review System (PNRS) of Part I. A–95 encourages, although it does not require, the establishment of a network of state, metropolitan and regional (nonmetropolitan) planning and development clearinghouses. The clearinghouses are review agencies, usually designated by the governor. A potential applicant for assistance under a program covered by A–95 is required to notify the appropriate state and regional (or metropolitan) clearinghouses of his intent to apply for a grant. The clearinghouses have 30 days in which to evaluate the proposal's relevance to any comprehensive area development plan, notify interested state and local agencies of the proposal, and arrange conferences to resolve conflicts. The clearinghouses have an additional 30 days to review the completed application. Their comments must accompany the proposal when it is submitted to the federal agency from which assistance is sought. Those federal agencies covered by A–95, in turn, may accept no application that has gone through the review process. The agencies are also responsible for notifying the clearinghouses which reviewed the application of any substantive action taken upon it— approval, rejection, return for amendment—within seven days after such action has been taken. Because such consultation on an informal basis to avoid conflict and to coordinate area plans is made before submission of the application for assistance to the federal agency, the A–95 PNRS has been termed an "early warning system." Figure 5–1 illustrates the notification and review process. By 1973 state clearinghouses had been established in every state. Four hundred and fifty substate clearinghouses, covering 85 percent of the country's population and almost 60 percent of its counties, had been designated.

Part II of Circular A–95 requires that agencies engaged in direct federal development projects consult with state and local officials to ensure project conformity to state, regional or local plans. There must be clear justification for exception when the projects do not conform. Part III affords governors a 45 day period to review state plans required by certain federal agencies as a condition for federal assistance, and to comment on their relationship to other state plans and programs. Part IV encourages the states to delineate planning and development districts to provide a consistent geographic base for the coordination of federal, state and local development programs. The circular was revised by the Office of Management and Budget in February 1971 to include an extensively expanded list of programs, with increased emphasis on those involving social and human resource development projects.

Because Circular A–95 encourages state and local initiative in the planning process, and provides an expanded role to state governors, it strengthens the federal system. To the extent that a project-by-project clearinghouse review of assistance requests eliminates conflict and duplication of effort, A–95 permits more efficient allocation of federal funds. And because the circular increases information flows among the several levels of government, states and localities can more effectively order their planning objectives and priorities and better integrate them into the exist-

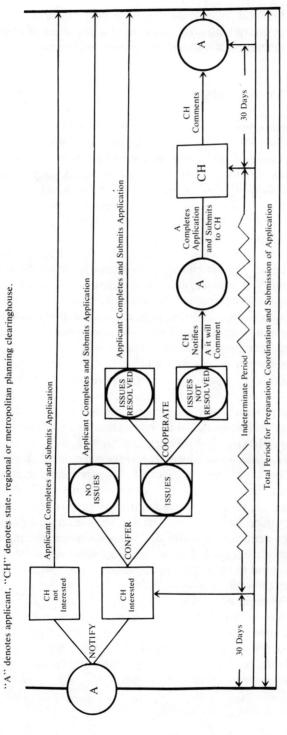

"A" denotes applicant, "CH" denotes state, regional or metropolitan planning clearinghouse.

Figure 5–1. A-95 Project Notification and Review Network.

ing system of federal grants and revenue sharing. However, the full potential of A–95 in coordinating the delivery of a broad range of government services has not yet been realized; the system can be improved in a number of ways.

IMPROVING THE SYSTEM

First, clearinghouses often lack sufficient staff and funds to perform their review functions adequately. OMB and the states should assure adequate no-strings funding of the review and comment function to the clearinghouses. States should provide increased technical, as well as financial, assistance to clearinghouse member governments, advise them on the availability of federal or state funds for regional purposes and provide professional staff to aid local officials in developing solutions to local and areawide planning problems.

Second, clearinghouses are suited to more than the coordination of the planning and development efforts of assistance agencies. In some states— e.g., Texas and Virginia—regional clearinghouses are actively involved in the development of comprehensive plans for two or more functional activities within their jurisdictions. With the advent of revenue sharing, the role of clearinghouses as participants in the specifics of planning and implementing development projects should be even more important. An expanded number of programs could be brought under the PNRS coordinating umbrella by state legislation requiring that all applications for federal and state assistance from state, regional and local organizations— as well as all programs—be subject to clearinghouse review.

Third, the notification duties of clearinghouses should be more carefully delineated and those of federal agencies more rigorously enforced. A–95 requires clearinghouses to inform state, regional or local agencies that may be affected by a proposed project of the applicant's intent to request assistance. But the circular establishes no minimum notification standard. OMB should issue guidelines to aid in the determination of agencies likely to be engaged in related projects. A clearinghouse receiving grant requests could then be required to notify any agencies administering established projects within its jurisdiction of the proposals. Also, because federal agencies also tend to shirk their notification responsibilities, OMB should require greater compliance on their part.

Fourth, the required review of state agency plans should be adhered to more carefully. A–95 permits state agencies to apply for federal planning and development assistance, but state agencies often serve on state clearinghouse boards and the reviewed are reluctant critics. Therefore, governors should be encouraged to require that state plans be subject to the same scrutiny as regional and local ones.

Finally, there is no A–95 review and comment procedure on the federal level to assure consistent federal agency assistance requirements. Perhaps too much of the burden of generalizing the activities of planning and development districts has been thrust upon the states; yet in the long run this may strengthen the position of the governors in the federal system, if they are ready, willing and able to seize the opportunity.

The key role of the governors in rural development planning has not received the attention it deserves. Interviews with persons closely connected with the Appalachian program have indicated again and again that the success of the program has been in direct proportion to the quantity and quality of the involvement of the relevant governors. It has been correctly argued that "the ability of the individual states to affect economic development is far greater than is usually appreciated. Even though the ultimate source of the funds may be the federal government, the fact is that the states are the principal mechanism by which government expenditures for domestic purposes are made."[1] But the governors must create meaningful planning units and compel the various federal agencies to coordinate their plans, programs and projects within the framework that they establish. Rural development efforts face enough difficulties without having to endure the inefficiencies of piecemeal and uncoordinated planning efforts.

A KENTUCKY CASE STUDY

The Setting

The recent history of Kentucky's Area Development Districts provides a good illustration of the opportunities that coordinated multicounty planning efforts represent for rural areas. According to Bureau of the Census definitions, the population of Kentucky is 47.7 percent rural, in contrast to the national figure of 26.5 percent. Moreover, substate planning in Kentucky has had an even greater rural orientation than its rural-urban population composition might suggest because the Louisville SMSA, which had a 1970 population of 827,000 has not participated fully in the ADD program. But even more persuasive reasons for examining the Kentucky case are the active gubernatorial support that has been given the ADD program and the planning innovations that have been introduced within its framework.

Recent History

In 1966 regional planning in Kentucky was uncoordinated; the Commonwealth had numerous development programs with inconsistent boundaries. They included the state department of commerce's 22 areas, OEO areas, a dozen vocational areas, child welfare areas, agricultural extension areas, health and mental health regions, area councils, department of highway regions, and others. Due to the proliferation of regional planning areas with differing boundaries and boards, county judges and mayors belonged to so many commissions and task forces that they often could make little sense of the big picture. In response, the director of the Kentucky Area Development Office was directed by Governor Breathitt to establish consistent boundaries for administering state programs.

A number of criteria were considered in the delineation of the substate planning areas, including retail sales areas as measured by consumer buying habits, communication networks of the public media, educational and vocational centers, labor market areas, transportation networks, population characteristics, industrialization patterns, agricultural patterns, resource development patterns, topographic features, remoteness from major metropolitan centers, activity levels of the development areas and areas of existing agencies. Although all these factors were considered, delineation of the substate planning areas was also strongly influenced by perceived "communities of interest—i.e., how well counties got along with one another and interacted; the district boundaries finally agreed upon in fact represented modifications of agricultural extension districts. It should be pointed out that while economic factors were not the sole criteria for delineation, the areas can be viewed appropriately as modified versions of the Basic Economic Research Areas discussed in the previous chapter.

Although the 15 substate planning districts (see Map 5–1) were established by the Breathitt administration in 1967, they were put into operation, funded and staffed during the administration of Governor Nunn. In 1968 he established the Kentucky Program Development Office (KPDO) as the statewide planning agency and the administrative center of the planning districts. When Circular A–95 was issued, KPDO was designated as the state clearinghouse and the boards of directors of the planning districts were designated as the area clearinghouses.

In Kentucky, federally sponsored multicounty areas generally conform to substate planning districts. This has been due largely to the initiative of the state in requiring federal agencies to conform. For example, KPDO initially had problems with the Economic Development Administration, which attempted to establish Economic Development Districts without regard to the substate planning districts. After numerous meetings with Bureau of the Budget officials in Washington and after implicit threats by KPDO officials to the effect that EDA would not be welcome unless it conformed to the state's planning districts, EDA finally agreed. In eastern Kentucky, the state districts and the Appalachian Regional Commission's Local Development Districts are coterminous.

Area Development Districts

In 1972, a ten year movement toward local government cooperation in partnership with the state culminated in the enactment, by the general

Map 5-1. Official Boundaries of the Kentucky Area Development Districts.

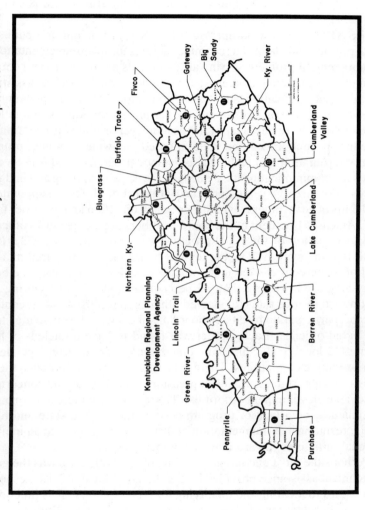

Source: Frankfort, Ky.: Commonwealth of Kentucky, Development Cabinet, 1974.

assembly, of a statutory base for the planning districts, now termed Area Development Districts (ADDs). Subsequently, the administrative reorganization of state government placed responsibility for coordination of ADD activities within the office for local government. (Eastern Kentucky's Appalachian Regional Commission Local Development District activities are coordinated at the state level by the governor's development cabinet, which works closely with the office for local government on matters pertaining to the region.) The new overall planning framework is shown in Figure 5–2.

The ADDs are now authorized to: (1) prepare, adopt and publish regional policies and plans and recommendations for their implementation; (2) promote mutual problem-solving arrangements among cities and counties for multijurisdictional concerns; (3) provide administrative assistance, federal grant application and procedural information and planning services, as requested by units of local government individually or jointly; (4) serve as the A–95 review agency; (5) assume responsibility for coordinating all federally encouraged and state initiated areawide planning, programming, coordination and technical assistance programs; and (6) serve as a means for communicating local needs to the state's planning and budgeting process. An Area Development District board of directors, appointed by local units of government, establishes policy direction and priorities for the staff. At least 51 percent of the board members are elected local officials.

An evaluation of the ADD program was undertaken in 1973.[2] It was found that in seven ADDs, the district board met the required minimum level of 51 percent elected local officials. In all but one case, the boards were composed of more than 45 percent elected officials. During 1973, meeting attendance rates for elected officials ranged from 30 percent to 72 percent; participation by citizen board members was closely related to that by elected officials. Each district was found to have a nucleus of highly committed local leadership, but some boards were overly dependent on their executive committees. There was a general need to broaden the base of district support to assure full expression of local needs and concerns and to achieve development priorities. The evaluation indicated that there continued to be a lack of program coordination at the state and federal levels, resulting in a fragmentation of district work effort and an inhibition on local initiatives toward addressing local needs.

Perhaps the most encouraging finding of the evaluation was the growth in technical assistance provided by the ADDs to local officials, especially with regard to locating and qualifying for federal grants. This function has been the cornerstone of ADD success and acceptance. During 1973 the ADDs were given funds for a program of management assistance involving a "roving city manager." ADD staffs can now, upon request, provide a

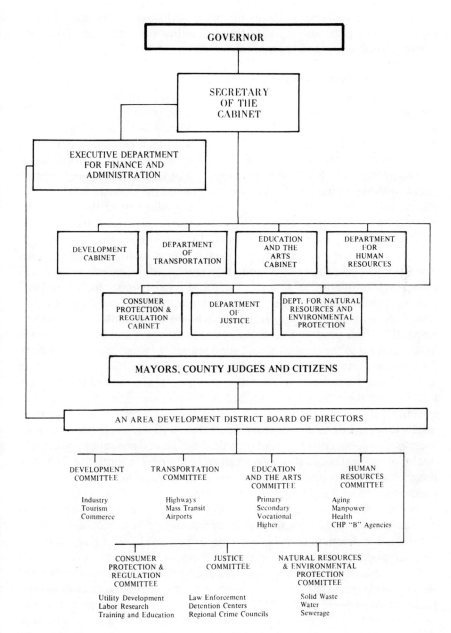

Figure 5–2. Kentucky State Government and Area Development District Organization.

wide range of assistance to local officials in such basic operating activities as budgeting, personnel administration, utility management and other common problem areas.

Integrated Grant Administration

A new Integrated Grant Administration (IGA) program will allow funding for all major programs carried out by the ADDs to be brought together within one application. For the first time, each ADD's planning, service and technical assistance can be designed and implemented as a part of an administratively uniform package rather than a product of scores of separate categorical projects. Such an innovation obviously could not be introduced without a climate of partnership between the state and the ADDs. Particularly noteworthy is the substantial commitment of the state's department of human resources both to the districts and to the use of IGA.

The unified IGA program is expected to benefit substate planning in numerous ways. It will eliminate the need for separate funding applications to each agency in the federal and state grant system, which in turn will promote coordination of federal, state and local funding for district activities. The disparity among various federal program funding cycles has tended to frustrate district efforts to achieve coordination within their respective work programs. Differences in fiscal years and funding periods have often led to the duplication of similar kinds of work in order to satisfy the requirements of individual funding agencies. Under IGA, all supporting agencies will fund the districts within a single fiscal year and the districts will receive their funds on a unified funding cycle. The office for local government is working with each of Kentucky's seven new cabinets to insure that all federally encouraged and state-initiated areawide planning, programming, coordination and technical assistance programs are carried out by—or coordinated through—ADDs. In the past, coordination of state program objectives and district programs has been difficult because of the fragmentation of ADD work programs. Under IGA, ADDs will be able to formulate unified work programs reflecting local needs and priorities as well as greater sensitivity to state program objectives. IGA also will increase the efficiency of program monitoring and will cut red tape by utilizing a common financial reporting system, a coordinated audit concept and a common completion report. A final clear benefit will be the saving of ADD professional staff time; less paper work means that greater effort can be devoted to providing assistance to local units of government. Obviously the scope of the IGA reform does not permit an overnight transition from the present system; it is estimated that the time required to implement the program will be five years, from fiscal year 1975 to fiscal year 1979. Nevertheless, many of the expected benefits should be realized before IGA is fully implemented.

Evaluation

A great deal of rhetoric concerning economic development surrounded the establishment of the ADDs, yet few of them have in fact had this orientation. In eastern Kentucky the Appalachian Regional Commission has only recently begun to have some real measure of success in making the region's ADDs more aware of economic development problems and potentials. In the western part of the state, management assistance to local officials and human resource programs has been the major concern.

The power of the county judge in rural Kentucky politics has proven to be an advantage to the ADD program—i.e., despotism has often turned out to be benevolent as well as efficient from a planning perspective. The Louisville area has not really been integrated into the total ADD framework because there is too much interagency bickering within the mini-UN metropolitan setting to devote attention to substate planning efforts. In contrast, communities in the more lagging rural areas of the state seem more willing to give up, or perhaps better, trade advantages vis-à-vis other communities in the hope that all will gain in the process.

While the Kentucky experience illustrates well the particular relevance of multicounty substate planning to rural areas, it even more clearly shows that the success of such planning depends on the positive commitment of the state, and, especially, of the governor.

SUMMARY AND CONCLUSIONS

The advent of substate regional planning and the A–95 review process is of vital significance for rural areas. Together they provide a potentially powerful vehicle for dealing constructively with problems which heretofore have too often been confronted in a piecemeal and uncoordinated manner, if at all. Commitment to these approaches varies widely among the states, though it tends to be greatest in states with relatively large nonmetropolitan populations. Despite pressure from the federal Office of Management and Budget for more and better coordination within the federal system, there is considerable foot dragging in many states. In most of these cases the governor has failed to exert positive leadership, for reasons ranging from sheer disinterest to unwillingness to strengthen the potential political power of small, competing local units of government.

Even in states where substate planning is taken quite seriously it is difficult for the A–95 review process to operate effectively because substate planning districts have not been able to agree on concrete priorities and objectives. Critics of revenue sharing have questioned the ability or interest of many local leaders and planning groups to identify local priority needs, much less the appropriate means for dealing with them. The same arguments may be urged against substate planning district boards. Often there is much to be gained by having higher level assistance in providing a perspective on local problems. The Appalachian Regional Commission has played a constructive role in this regard, as have the governors in some states. Nevertheless, it is difficult to compel compliance at the substate level.

In the context of the present study it is particularly relevant to point out the relative lack of integration of manpower programs into substate regional planning. It is curious that although many rural districts seem eager to attract firms—i.e., to increase the local demand for labor—few seem equally interested in upgrading the quality of the local labor force. In connection with the present study, rural manpower officials in 31 states were asked whether or not manpower planning was carried out in the context of substate regional planning; the officials also were invited to comment on the consequences of any discrepancies in this regard. The replies clearly indicated that rural manpower planning is only rarely integrated with more general substate planning efforts, and even then the marriage may not be successful. In the great majority of cases the officials communicated attitudes of ignorance, indifference, futility or hostility. In some instances these attitudes may well have been perfectly reasonable responses to the quality of substate planning efforts. Nevertheless, there is evidence that manpower and substate regional planning can be integrated to their mutual benefit. Despite the fact that Kentucky's ADD program provides many constructive insights, the experience of her neighbor to the south provides more instruction in a manpower perspective. The following chapter discusses the nature and significance of major new federal manpower legislation and of its application in Tennessee.

NOTES

[1] Alfred S. Eichner, *State Development Agencies and Employment Expansion* (Ann Arbor: University of Michigan and Wayne State University Institute of Labor and Industrial Relations, 1970), p. 2.

[2] *Kentucky's Area Development Districts: Evaluation and Progress, 1973* (Frankfort, Ky.: Commonwealth Office for Local Government, 1974). The Jefferson ADD (Louisville) was not included in the evaluation.

[3] For further details, see *Integrated Planning Administrative Program* (Frankfort, Ky.: Commonwealth Executive Department for Finance and Administration, 1974).

Chapter Six

CETA and Manpower Planning in Nonmetropolitan Areas

THE COMPREHENSIVE EMPLOYMENT AND TRAINING ACT OF 1973

Preliminary Reform Efforts

Large scale federal involvement with manpower programs began with the enactment of the Manpower Development and Training Act (MDTA) in 1962, as well as the manpower provisions of the Economic Opportunity Act of 1964. Appropriations under these acts supported numerous different national categorical grant programs. MDTA institutional and on-the-job training provisions had a number of variants; there were three Neighborhood Youth Corps programs, four separate Public Service Careers programs, Operation Mainstream, Job Corps and the Concentrated Employment Program (CEP). Another categorical program to provide public employment was added with the passage of the Emergency Employment Act of 1971. These categorical programs had their own client groups, project designs, standards and methods of operation. Most of them operated on the basis of some 10,000 direct grants and contracts between the U.S. Department of Labor and public and private organizations.

Although many unemployed and underemployed persons were helped by these programs, separate project administration was often costly, confusing, duplicative and inefficient. Separate guidelines written in Washington did not permit much flexibility in the use of funds from the many categorical programs. Local officials and individuals who sought assistance in this setting had to deal with many layers of federal bureaucracy. Moreover, it was widely felt that program guidelines formulated in Washington could not foresee and were not responsive to varied local problems and needs.

In response to this situation, President Nixon first proposed comprehensive manpower legislation in 1969. The bill he proposed would have decentralized decisionmaking to state and local governments and would have eliminated categorical restrictions. A similar bill was submitted to Congress a year and a half later. Although these bills were not enacted, the relevant debates and hearings indicated widespread and growing sympathy for their principal objectives, which were to (1) unify federally supported manpower service efforts, (2) free city, county and state budgets from fund-matching and maintenance of effort encumbrances and permit state and local flexibility in meeting manpower needs, and (3) vest the power to shape manpower programs in those levels of government closest to the problems. By 1973, both the House and Senate were working on bills to decentralize and decategorize manpower programs, a process already being carried out to a limited extent by executive branch administrative methods. The result of these efforts was the Comprehensive Employment and Training Act of 1973, which President Nixon signed in late December.

Principal Provisions of CETA

According to Section 2 of the act, the general objective of CETA is "to provide job training and employment opportunities for economically disadvantaged, unemployed, and underemployed persons, and to assure that training and other services lead to maximum employment opportunities and enhance self-sufficiency by establishing a flexible and decentralized system of Federal, State, and local programs."

CETA largely eliminated the numerous categorical programs authorized under earlier legislation. Whereas manpower programs had been operated on a project-by-project basis through separate sponsors, the secretary of labor now makes block grants to some 500 local and state prime sponsors who are supposed to plan and operate manpower programs to meet local needs. The secretary is responsible for assuring that prime sponsors comply with the provisions of CETA and he has authority over programs for certain target groups such as Indians, migrant workers and criminal offenders. The secretary also is responsible for the Job Corps program and for research, training, evaluation and other functions best carried out at the national level. Up to 20 percent of CETA funds are available to the secretary for national activities; however, the great majority of appropriations are for formula distribution to state and local governments serving as prime sponsors.

With a few exceptions, a prime sponsor can be a state; a unit of local government with a population of 100,000 or more; or a combination of local units, one of which has a population of 100,000 or more. In most rural areas, services under CETA are provided by the state, operating as a "balance-of-state" prime sponsor. In order to qualify as a prime sponsor, a state, locality or other unit must submit a notice of intent to apply for prime sponsorship to the relevant assistant regional director for manpower (there are ten multistate regions) and to the governor. The applicant also must submit a comprehensive manpower plan covering the area to be served and specifying the services to be provided. Assurances are required that programs will be administered properly and that services will reach those most in need of them. Each local prime sponsor must establish a planning council; most state prime sponsors must also create a state manpower services council. CETA further requires the participation of community-based organizations in program planning and it calls for objective consideration of the use of existing federal, state, local and private organizations. Planning councils—with representatives from the client community, the employment service, education and training agencies, business, labor, and, where appropriate, agriculture—not only recommend plans, procedures and goals, but also monitor programs and evaluate manpower efforts in the light of local needs. CETA requires administrative controls and accounting procedures and specifies that records be kept to which the Department of Labor will have access. To improve efficiency, the Manpower Administration conducts extensive technical assistance programs for prime sponsors. Despite the prime sponsor's accountability to the Department of Labor, it is hoped that, in the spirit of decentralization, the final control over poor judgment and inefficiency will be exercised by the voters, since prime sponsors are elected officials. In general, then, states and localities will determine what mix of programs best serves their needs, though Department of Labor technical assistance is available for planning, financial management, organization and staffing, proposal preparation, and grant administration. The prime sponsor may, for example, establish new youth programs or continue existing ones such as Neighborhood Youth Corps projects. However, the group served, the name of the project and the extent of services are all up to the prime sponsor.

Eighty percent of CETA Title I funds are to be distributed to prime sponsors according to the following formula: 50 percent is based on the manpower allotment in the previous fiscal year, 37.5 percent is based on the number of unemployed in the state and 12.5 percent is allotted according to the number of adults in low income families. There is a limit on the percentage increase or decrease in funds for each jurisdiction compared with its prior year's funding level. Up to 1 percent of the money distributed among the states by this formula is available for state manpower services councils.

Of the remaining 20 percent of Title I money, 5 percent is available to develop combinations of local government units to serve as program sponsors, 5 percent is available for grants to provide needed vocational education services, 4 percent is to help states make comprehensive plans and coordinate manpower services and the remaining funds are to be used at the discretion of the secretary of labor.

Title II of CETA provides for programs of transitional public service employment in areas with a 6.5 percent or higher rate of unemployment for three consecutive months. Program sponsors may be prime sponsors qualified under Title I or Indian tribes. Applications for Title II funds must contain specific plans for a public service employment program to serve persons who have been unemployed for at least 30 days. To the extent feasible, the programs should develop new careers, open opportunities for career advancement and enable people in the program to move into other public or private employment. Priority is to be given to veterans and to the most severely disadvantaged among the unemployed. Eighty percent of Title II funds are allocated according to an unemployment yardstick. The remainder are to be distributed at the discretion of the secretary of labor.

It may finally be noted that although the initial CETA legislation is comprehensive in many respects, it still accounted for only two-fifths of the then current annual $4.8 billion in outlays for manpower services. Excluded are important manpower-related programs such as veterans' assistance, services for welfare recipients and the disabled, and placement activities of the federal-state employment service.[1]

Because of high and rising unemployment levels, President Ford, in December 1974, signed the Emergency Jobs and Unemployment Assistance Act, under which unemployed and underemployed persons were hired for jobs providing needed public services. Where feasible, such persons were given training and services for employment in improving environmental quality, health care, education, recreation, pollution control, conservation and other areas of community betterment. The legislation created a new Title VI of CETA authorizing the appropriation of $2.5 billion for fiscal year 1975 for this title. Any funds not obligated by the end of the fiscal year (June 30, 1975) were made available through December 31, 1975. Prime sponsors qualified under Title I were made eligible to apply for Title VI funds.

Not less than 90 percent of Title VI funds were allocated as follows: 50 percent in proportion to each area's share of unemployed persons, 25 percent in proportion to the area's share of unemployed persons in excess of 4.5 percent of the labor force and 25 percent among areas of substantial—6.5 percent for three consecutive months—unemployment as defined in Title II. The remaining 10 percent or less of Title VI funds are for discretionary use by the secretary of labor, taking into account changes in unemployment rates.

To the extent feasible, preference in hiring for Title VI jobs was given to experienced workers who had exhausted all unemployment compensation or were not eligible for it, and experienced workers who had been without a job for 15 weeks or longer. Moreover, various provisions of the public employment program under Title II were waived to provide job opportunities in areas with unemployment rates of 7 percent or more.

CETA and Rural Areas

In the first two chapters of this study it was argued that the problems of rural areas were neglected under federal manpower legislation prior to CETA. There is little in CETA to indicate that this situation will be any different in the future. Needless to say, many legislators from rural areas were opposed to the 100,000 minimum population criterion for qualification as a prime sponsor. To them, CETA meant that if a locality has more than 100,000 inhabitants then local government knows best; if there are not this many people then local government really does not know best.[2] No doubt there is a measure of hypocrisy in arguing for decentralization on the basis of the virtue of government close to the people, but then excluding even some SMSAs on the implicit assumption that local government in small SMSAs and nonmetropolitan areas simply cannot handle manpower programs. The implicit assumption that the purpose and clientele associated with CETA are relevant only to metropolitan areas may be a consequence of the low visibility of small town and rural residents who need manpower services. However, the initial difficulties experienced by prime sponsors (and federal officials) with respect to the organization, financing, contracting and local delivery of CETA manpower services suggests that the situation might have been worse if nonmetropolitan areas were themselves prime sponsors.

> Lack of familiarity with previous manpower legislation, programs, administrative and operating practices, including interagency coordination, added immensely to the problems of time constraints in rural areas often starting from "scratch." In some states where the Governor, as prime sponsor for CETA programs in rural areas, decentralized responsibility to county commissioners, general revenue sharing (already experienced) was often confused with manpower revenue sharing calling for compliance with specific legislative requisites of delivery of services and financial accountability. In these situations, rural local government often lacked not only professional staff competence to develop a rural manpower service plan, but had no knowledge of the Coordinated Area Manpower Planning System (CAMPS) or the subsequent coordinating organizations such as the Ancillary Manpower Planning Council.[3]

Louis Levine also has pointed out that despite the difficult problems involved in the transition to local delivery of CETA manpower services

> urban areas do have advantages over rural ones. Generally, the prime sponsor can exercise options as to the best deliverers of manpower services. At least three local agencies can compete: The Employment Service, the Community Action Agency, and private groups such as the Urban League. These options do not always exist in rural areas. Often there is no local employment office in a rural county, while other rural or agricultural organizations such as

the Cooperative Extension Service have little or no experience or knowledge in the manpower field.[4]

Because manpower services other than labor exchange and placement services are central to CETA, the extent to which the employment service can play an innovative role in rural areas is highly uncertain. The employment service can provide, and in a number of states has provided, rural manpower services, but in some instances other deliverers have competed successfully. Some CETA prime sponsors and groups administering rural manpower programs have criticized the employment service's rigid operating procedures and practices; it has been claimed that insufficient authority has been delegated to permit changes in local organization structures and staff functions, and that the employment service is too concerned with other statutory obligations to give proper attention to CETA clients.

A particularly vexing problem for rural areas is the use of unemployment rates in determining need for CETA services, and thus funding. "Based on earlier experience with public employment programs, rural areas are unlikely to establish claims for participation in these programs on any considerable scale. A major barrier is inadequate labor market information and inability to measure the unemployment rate."[5] Reliance on the unemployment rate as a measure of economic well-being is especially unrealistic in the rural South. For example, a study of the definition of depressed areas found that in 1960 the South accounted for nearly all of the 300 lowest-ranking counties in the nation in terms of percent of families with income under $2000. In contrast, the 300 counties with the highest unemployment rates were rather widely scattered throughout the country, though regional concentrations of unemployment were found in New England, Appalachia, the Upper Great Lakes and the Pacific Northwest. The only section of the country to have the dubious distinction of being among the worst-off places in terms of both unemployment and low income was central Appalachia.[6] It also may be noted that the unemployment rate for blacks in the rural South prior to 1863 was extremely low; despite some revisionist views, few would claim that unemployment rates now or then accurately reflect this group's economic status.

Given, then, that CETA is essentially metropolitan in orientation, the fact remains that the quality of the residual, or balance-of-state, manpower programs depends heavily on how they are administered by the respective governors. Neither CETA itself nor Department of Labor regulations provide much guidance to local governments in essentially rural areas. However, it is clear that local officials will have to develop working relations with their state house rather than the Department of Labor. As prime sponsors for balance-of-state areas the governors are treated just as city and county prime sponsors; no special role is provided for elected local officials in rural areas. Although the governors are supposed to make an equitable distribution of funds, numerous problems already discussed may make it difficult for local governments to determine whether they are receiving funds commensurate with their needs. Moreover, while CETA specifies how funds are to be allocated to prime sponsors it does not require such a breakdown for rural jurisdictions. Nor does it require that elected rural officials be named to manpower advisory councils. Thus, governors are given wide discretion and it is not surprising that emerging state structures reflect a variety of responses and varying degrees of decentralization.

At the end of the previous chapter it was pointed out that Tennessee has made considerable progress in implementing substate district planning for nonmetropolitan areas and that manpower programs have been closely integrated into this effort. Because so many people in the rural South belong to the "economically disadvantaged, unemployed, and under-employed" target population for CETA programs, and because Tennessee has attempted to create responsive balance-of-state manpower institutions and programs, it is instructive to consider its recent experience in some detail.

CETA IN NONMETROPOLITAN TENNESSEE

The Development District Framework

Tennessee's nine development districts were designated by the state planning commission and given legal status by the state assembly in 1965. Before a district was designated, three-fourths of the county judges and three-fourths of the mayors in the area had to vote their approval. In each district local leaders use a common planning staff to (1) develop plans and formulate programs to increase economic growth and reduce unemployment, (2) encourage mutual cooperation among member governments and (3) develop and support common interests in relationships with the state and federal governments. The district governing board includes county judges, mayors and county representatives appointed by the county judges. An executive committee, including a member from each district county, oversees the planning staff, which is composed of an executive director elected by the governing board and a number of professional persons with skills in planning, promotion of economic development and administration. The planning staff assists local governments in identifying and participating in federal and state programs that can be used in overcoming development problems. The districts serve as regional clearinghouses in the A–95 review process.

District financial support is based on a per capita assessment to member counties. Cities and other public or private sources can provide up to one-half of the county's share. State law limits dues to 10 cents per capita and provides that no county may pay more than $7500. The state matches—on a two-to-one basis—up to $60,000, the funds raised locally by county and city governments. These funds may in turn be matched by federal planning and development money on a multiple basis. Thus, $10,000 in funds raised locally may be supplemented by, say, $10,000 in state funds and $60,000 in federal planning funds, for a total district staff budget of $80,000.

State agencies have been encouraged to coordinate their local activities with the staffs of the districts, and they have been required to align their planning and service area boundaries with district boundaries. In addition, some state agencies have internal policies of coordination with district staffs because the latter often prepare functional development plans relating to state responsibilities, and vice versa. Among these state agencies are the department of transportation, the department of economic and community development, comprehensive health planning, emergency medical services and the department of employment security.

Balance-of-State CETA Planning

The administrative framework for CETA planning was provided by Executive Order No. 36, signed by Governor Dunn in May 1974. It created a Manpower Services Council (MSC) to oversee all manpower activities in the state. The chairman of the MSC is the governor; the vice chairman is the commissioner of the department of economic and community development. The MSC also includes representatives of prime sponsors, state agencies, manpower services clients and area subcouncils. Its function is to monitor state services for their availability to clients and prime sponsors, for their responsiveness to client needs and to state manpower requirements, and for adequacy in terms of service quality and the proportion of the target group served. On the basis of its review and monitoring activity the MSC makes recommendations to prime sponsors, state agencies, the governor and the general public concerning ways to improve the effectiveness of manpower programs in meeting state needs and CETA requirements.

There are seven prime sponsors in Tennessee: (1) the city of Memphis and Shelby County, (2) Nashville metro government (Nashville and Davidson County have formed a metropolitan government), (3) Chattanooga, (4) Hamilton County outside of Chattanooga, (5) Knoxville, (6) Knox County outside of Knoxville and (7) the governor for the balance-of-state.

The state of Tennessee, as prime sponsor for balance-of-state areas, was required by Section 104 of CETA to appoint a Manpower Planning Council. The chairman and vice chairman are the same as those for the MSC. Other members include state agency representatives, client community representatives and the chairmen of the nine manpower planning subcouncils. The Manpower Planning Council submits to the governor recommendations regarding program goals, policies and procedures; it monitors and evaluates all CETA-funded activities in balance-of-state areas. However, the council is only advisory and final decisions with respect to its recommendations are made by the prime sponsor.

The nine manpower planning subcouncils are a part of, or an extension of, the balance-of-state Manpower Planning Council. The subcouncils are geographically coterminous with the development districts. Although the subcouncils and development districts are legally separate and autonomous bodies they cooperate closely. The chairman of each development district is also a member of the region's subcouncil and manpower programs are explicitly integrated with area planning and economic development efforts. Each subcouncil chairman is designated by the chief elected officials of the units of government comprising the respective planning areas. Membership on the subcouncil is limited to those agencies actually involved in the delivery of manpower programs or agencies that provide supportive services. The composition of a typical subcouncil might include, in addition to the chairman, representatives from the human resource agency (the operational component of the development district in the delivery of human resource development programs), the department of employment security, vocational education, the department of public welfare, the department of public health, vocational rehabilitation, the community action agency, the local educational cooperative and other manpower-related agencies common to the planning area.

Prior to CETA, manpower activities in Tennessee were operated by different agencies without much overall coordination. Federal exhortations concerning the need for comprehensive planning were honored more in principle than in fact. Cooperative Area Manpower Planning System (CAMPS) councils did not exercise much initiative but rather served to sanction the existing system. The Tennessee Manpower Council was created as the state counterpart of the CAMPS in 1972 and was made part of the employment security office. After CETA, the Manpower Council was replaced by the Manpower Service Council, which was placed in the department of economic and community development.

Before CETA manpower planning and programs were not channeled through the development districts, which merely served as a basis of classification for programs. The principal barriers to coordinated, comprehensive manpower planning at the regional level were agency resistances to change and a formidable and confusing array of guidelines for federal funding of programs. The principal impact of CETA in Tennessee has been to strengthen manpower planning at the regional level by compelling relevant agencies to coordinate their efforts within each development district. Although the Manpower Planning Council is formally responsible for the administration of balance-of-state manpower programs, it in fact customarily rubber-stamps the programs developed at the district level by the manpower subcouncils. The issue is not so much one of inertia at the state level as recognition that district level planning is essential in a state as heterogeneous as Tennessee. In this sense, the "local area knows best" rationale for CETA has been justified.

Another noteworthy feature of manpower planning in Tennessee is the high degree of support and cooperation that local governments within development districts have given to areawide identification of needs and programs for dealing with them. Elected officials are primarily responsible for articulating priority needs; the manpower subcouncils are primarily responsible for developing responsive plans. Existing manpower-related agencies within the districts are expected to provide the resources necessary for program implementation; the state provides technical assistance, usually through a regional planner. As pointed out earlier, the districts are authorized to create human resource agencies to provide appropriate delivery systems.

A major reason for the high degree of serious local support for both economic development planning and manpower planning at the district level has been a feeling among local officials that nonmetropolitan areas have *not* been relegated to secondary status in relation to metropolitan prime sponsors. Manpower and area development planning at the state level has deliberately avoided growth center (and service center) approaches, which are unpopular among nonmetropolitan leaders who feel that they unfairly ignore large segments of the rural population. The feeling at the state level is that if development programs were designed around a growth center strategy, planning problems would be compounded.

Strong local identification in nonmetropolitan Tennessee has also been largely responsible for the fact that there is only one CETA consortium in the state; rural counties are extremely reluctant to form consortia with neighboring SMSAs because they assume, rightly or wrongly, that their needs will be ignored in favor of those of the SMSAs. Moreover, given a long history of outmigration from certain areas of the state, and actual decline of population in some nonmetropolitan counties, development programs which might increase geographic mobility—especially of better educated and skilled persons—are viewed with hostility. Thus, state manpower planning makes no explicit effort to match workers in areas of labor surplus with jobs in areas of labor shortage. The emphasis is rather on developing employment opportunities in rural areas so that people do not have to move away to find work; and local officials in rural areas resent metropolitan influence and prefer to formulate their own development strategies.

At present, the state Manpower Planning Council is concentrating on generating more and better data on nonmetropolitan areas. In the past, data collection focused on SMSAs, but planning officials now realize that their efforts could be seriously misdirected because of an inadequate data base for nonmetropolitan areas. Some rural counties appear to be economically well off because many people who live in them commute to work in SMSAs; however, large segments of the population of these commuter counties are in fact disadvantaged and unemployed or underemployed. Efforts are being made to collect data that will make it easier to isolate and identify groups in need of manpower services. Separate information also is being compiled on the many seasonal farm workers in Tennessee.

The Manpower Planning Council is attempting to specify the availability of manpower services in each development district so that duplication of effort by various agencies can be identified and eliminated. Many programs were unsuccessful in the past because of interagency competition for clients and consequent high administrative costs. It is strongly felt in Tennessee that successful manpower planning requires a single delivery system. Interested agencies or groups may submit bids on projects and contracts are awarded on a competitive basis. Human resource agencies are operational components of the development districts; in six districts they implement manpower and manpower-related programs. The employment security service operates intake, job training and placement services in three districts; however, its role is relatively subdued in rural Tennessee in these regards because the agency is not very popular at the local level. The employment service has a reputation for ignoring local needs and for failure to coordinate its activities with those of the development districts.

Tennessee manpower planning officials feel that in a national context the state has received a "fair share" of CETA Title I funds and that there has been an equitable division of these funds between metropolitan and nonmetropolitan areas within Tennessee. On the other hand, there is considerable resentment concerning the distribution of Title II and Title VI public service employment money. It is felt that Northeastern and Western states—and especially large SMSAs within these states—have received an unjustifiably large share of the total funding. One official alleged that New York City alone received more money for public service employment under CETA than did all of the Southeastern states combined.

On the basis of current tendencies, future state level manpower planning in Tennessee will continue to encourage training for occupations where shortages of skilled workers are indicated. The agricultural bias still found in vocational education programs in some rural areas will no doubt be modified in favor of training for employment in industry or the tertiary sector. Problems of cyclical unemployment are much less severe in rural areas of Tennessee than in the state's SMSAs; unemployment and under-employment have persisted for so many decades in rural areas that the effects of a national recession simply do not have a dramatic impact. Viewed in this context, it is appropriate that balance-of-state manpower planning emphasizes longer run human resource development needs and employment opportunities.

At the state level, manpower planning in Tennessee provides reasonable justification for CETA's decentralization rationale. But the real test of the efficiency of decentralization is occurring at the development district level, for state manpower planning is essentially the sum of the activities of the metropolitan prime sponsors and the various balance-of-state manpower planning subcouncils. Among the latter, the Upper Cumberland and First Tennessee subcouncils are regarded by informed outside observers as being particularly effective.

Upper Cumberland Manpower Planning Subcouncil

The Upper Cumberland Development District (UCDD) is comprised of 14 counties located in north central Tennessee (see Map 6–1). It has a total land area of over 5000 square miles and includes three different physiographic regions. The western portion, about 29 percent of the UCDD, lies within the Central Basin and has an average elevation of about 500 feet. Above the Central Basin is the Highland Rim, a section of rolling tableland accounting for 31 percent of the UCDD's total area. The remaining 40 percent of the district is in the Cumberland Plateau and ranges in elevation from 2000 to 3500 feet. Throughout the district there are numerous parks, recreation areas, lakes and tourist attractions.

There are two distinct labor market areas; their respective centers are Putnam County (Cookeville) and Warren County (McMinnville). These were the only counties with net inmigration during the 1960s. The district as a whole had net outmigration of 5536 persons, but its population grew by 10,385, to 193,745, as a consequence of natural increase of 15,921 persons. Although the median age has remained fairly constant in Tennessee since 1950, it has steadily increased in the UCDD from 24.7 years in 1950 (less than the corresponding state figure of 27.3 years) to 30.9 years in 1970 (more than the state's corresponding 28.1 years). People are living to an older age and many young people are continuing to migrate to other parts of Tennessee and to Northern cities to secure employment, a common phenomenon since the Second World War. Only 2 percent of the district population is nonwhite—two counties have no black population. Of the UCDD's 53,064 families, 14,609 were classified as below the poverty level at the time of the 1970 census. With an average family size of 3.44 persons, this indicated that about 50,000 persons, or 27.5 percent of population, was

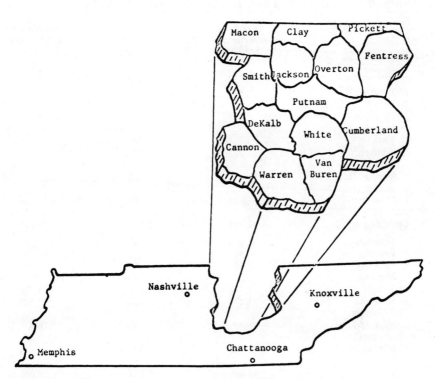

Map 6–1.   The Upper Cumberland Development District.

in poverty. Another 34,366 persons fell within the near-poverty range, which means that nearly 44 percent of the district's population was below or near the poverty level.

The client groups to be served by CETA manpower services in the Upper Cumberland, and the estimated number to be served in fiscal year 1976, are shown in Table 6–1. Most of the disadvantaged target population

Table 6–1.   Upper Cumberland Client Groups To Be Served and Number To Be Served in Each Group, Fiscal Year 1976

Client Group	Number Needing Service	Number to be Served	Balance Needing Service
A. Unemployed	3,610	653	2,957
1. Veterans	664	200	464
2. Females	1,480	288	1,192
3. Heads of household	1,495	376	1,119
4. Youth	311	100	211
5. Welfare recipients	285	200	85
6. Migrant farm workers	INA[1]	100	INA
7. Minorities	70	44	26
B. Underemployed	40,371	1,564	38,807
1. Veterans	806	243	563
2. Females	16,511	322	16,189
3. Heads of household	16,554	416	16,138
4. Youth	3,485	115	3,370
5. Welfare recipients	3,174	286	2,888
6. Migrant farm workers	INA	100	INA
7. Minorities	743	300	443
C. Economically disadvantaged	18,868	783	18,085
1. Veterans	321	100	221
2. Females	8,158	250	7,908
3. Heads of household	8,214	210	8,004
4. Youth	1,692	600	1,092
5. Welfare recipients	1,575	70	1,505
6. Migrant farm workers	INA	50	INA
7. Minorities	327	80	247

Source: Upper Cumberland Manpower Planning Subcouncil, "Fiscal Year 1976 Manpower Plan," p. 26.

1. INA indicates information not available.

has either no previous work record, a poor work record or no marketable skills. Those with work records and a marketable skill frequently have bad work habits—e.g., constant absence from work, being late to work or leaving a job without just cause. Under such conditions the employer is only being realistic in not wanting to hire these persons.

However, unrealistic employer hiring specifications are apparent in dealing with the veteran, the youth and those displaced workers over 45 years. The employer is trying, in many cases, to hire the returning veteran at a pay rate below that at which he can make a decent living. The employer is also setting educational requirements above the requirements that are needed to perform the particular job. The employer is not always providing proper working conditions for his employees. These conditions, along with a low rate of pay, do not make it practical for the veteran to take this employment.

The employer is reluctant to hire the worker over 45 years. He prefers the younger worker, especially if he is having to share in a company insurance program. By using the younger employee, the group insurance premium, based on the average age of the employees, is at a cheaper rate. Therefore, the employer states that he will not hire anyone with long hair. Many veterans are subjected to the long hair specifications.[7]

Other manpower-relevant problems in the UCDD include lack of skills among disadvantaged groups, low wages, difficulty in organizing the large number of females employed in the garment industry (union restrictions have no effect on local labor market conditions because so few workers are organized), seasonal unemployment in the construction and tourist industries, lack of adequate day care facilities, and transportation inadequacies. With the exception of a four county minibus service funded by the Office of Economic Opportunity, taxis have provided the only mode of public transportation in the UCDD and their cost is prohibitive to the target population. Some target group members try to provide their own transportation by owning two or three old cars and stripping parts from one to keep another running, but even then the auto which runs is not dependable.

In addition to careful and realistic analyses of the labor force, manpower planning also benefits from close cooperation with the development district in projecting local employment needs by occupation. While the district attempts to expand employment opportunities, the manpower subcouncil pursues three principal service goals: (1) to change the attitudes and work habits of target groups; (2) to raise the educational and skill levels for certain target groups through basic education and vocational training; and (3) to raise the employability levels of young people, older workers and unskilled workers. The subcouncil maintains a complete inventory of current program efforts and it regularly assesses their performance. The client flow plan used in the UCDD is shown in Figure 6–1.

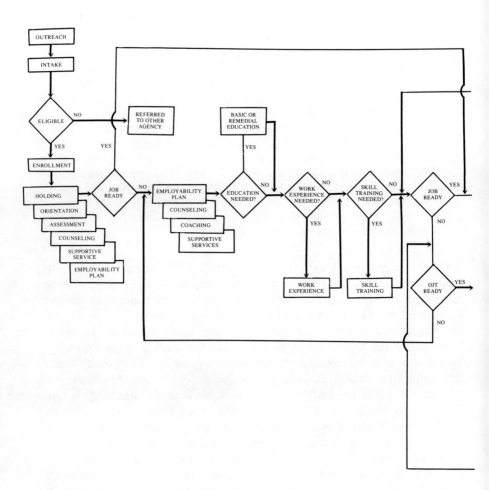

Figure 6–1. Upper Cumberland Comprehensive Employment and Training Act—Client Flow Plan.

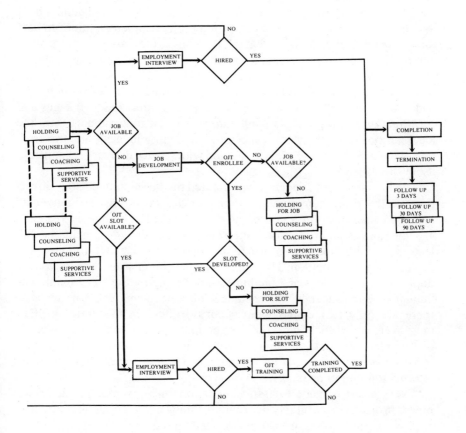

Coordination of area development and manpower planning in the UCDD is assured by the fact that the chairman of the manpower planning subcouncil is also the executive director of the UCDD. Moreover, the person in question, Dr. Donald Wakefield, has received national recognition for the positive leadership he has exerted in the Upper Cumberland area.

Prior to CETA, approximately $5 million annually was expended on district manpower projects; the current funding level is only about $2.5 million. Nevertheless, local manpower officials are encouraged because CETA has greatly increased the effectiveness of manpower planning, both in defining objectives and in program and project implementation. In part this is a result of the authority that CETA gives to local areas to define their manpower needs and to decide on the best service delivery systems. However, the success of manpower efforts in the UCDD also are due to a combination of other factors, including the presence of a highly motivated and experienced planning staff, the existence of interagency linkages and coordination in program planning and delivery, strong support from the local political establishment (especially the county judges), and the creation of a human resource agency charged with service delivery responsibility in the district.

The human resource agency was created by the subcouncil after efforts to have the three community action agencies in the district deliver all manpower services on a coordinated basis failed. The human resource agency handles all aspects of manpower services delivery, including collection of labor market information, intake, counseling, training, job placement and evaluation. This approach cuts administrative costs, avoids duplication of services and facilitates monitoring by the subcouncil. The human resource agency has assumed job placement functions because there are only two employment security offices in the entire UCDD; moreover, these offices have not been cooperative within the framework of district planning. Indeed, employment security even refuses to the human resource agency the use of its scanners for viewing microfiches containing information on job openings.

Every effort is made to assure that economic development and manpower projects are equitably distributed among district counties. Counties with small populations are not overlooked, and counties with particularly severe problems are at times given favorable treatment. Although Cookeville, McMinnville and Crossville are growing relatively rapidly, there is no attempt to channel more funds into them for their promotion as growth centers. This accords with the general policy of trying to make each county feel that, over the long run at least, it is getting its "fair share" of district funds. The human resource agency maintains an information agency in every county and makes substantial efforts to inform residents about available services. Considerable emphasis has been placed on cooperative education and training between high schools and the vocational schools in the district. The school boards in three counties have pooled their resources to provide support for a common vocational school. As a result of these and related efforts, the question of equity of access to manpower services for rural residents is not an issue in the UCDD.

During the early 1970s some district residents were trained for job openings outside of the district. However, most of these trainees were reluctant to move and the few who did returned to their homes within a year. Although strong family and community ties seem to preclude labor mobility programs, the subcouncil is considering a pilot project in which three or four families would be encouraged to move together. There is not much optimism concerning the chances for success because people who want to migrate do so on their own initiative, while those who leave merely because there are supportive services are likely to return because of psychological pulls toward home.

The need to improve rural transportation systems is clearly recognized at both the state level and in the UCDD. The state has no concrete plans in this regard because of the high cost that would be involved. The UCDD has applied for a $4 million grant from the Department of Transportation to implement a project within the district; the application is pending at this writing. If implemented, major trunk connections would be established among all 14 county seats. Feeder lines using 16 minibuses would be tied into the trunk lines. In the absence of large federal or state subsidies the UCDD cannot even attempt to overcome rural transportation deficiencies and many rural residents will continue to be restricted in their ability to take advantage of training and employment opportunities.

First Tennessee Manpower Planning Subcouncil

The First Tennessee-Virginia Development District is located in extreme northeastern Tennessee and contains a portion of southwestern Virginia (see Map 6–2). The nine county area, which covers nearly 3500 square miles, has rough farm land and rugged mountains on its western edge; on its eastern fringe is the mountainous Cherokee National Forest. Urban and industrial growth have been pronounced in the Great Appalachian Valley, which runs through the middle of the district. Between 1960 and 1970 district population increased from 383,299 to 415,102; it is projected to grow to about 520,000 in 1980 and to about 680,000 by the end of the century. This is in marked contrast to the 1950s, when there was net outmigration, growth was slow and five counties actually lost population (only one lost population during the 1960s). The demographic shift began during the mid-1960s and coincided with a period of rapid industrial expan-

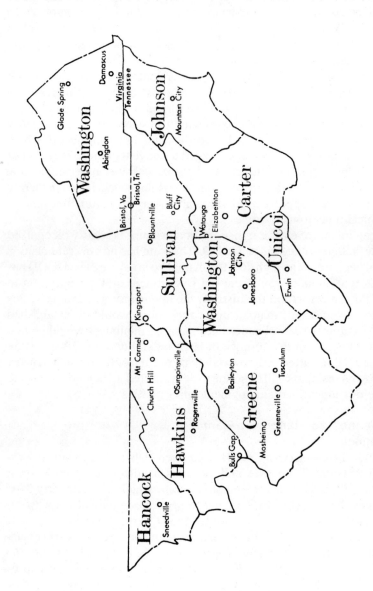

Map 6–2. First Tennessee-Virginia Development District.

sion and the creation of thousands of new jobs. Increasingly, farm families have moved into the urban centers of Bristol, Johnson City and Kingsport or into the areas between them.

Until the mid-1960s individual efforts by communities of upper east Tennessee and portions of southwest Virginia failed to make a dent in serious development problems which most of them shared in common. Competition for available federal resources was the rule rather than the exception. The cooperative regional approach adopted under pressure from both the state and federal governments gave local elected officials an opportunity to work effectively together for the first time. As in the UCDD, they discovered they had much in common; from this beginning county judges and mayors now work regularly together in defining common problems and setting consensus goals and priorities for improving the region. The initial objectives of district planning were to build up the infrastructure necessary to attract industry and to upgrade labor force skills.

Industrial development has been quite successful. Manufacturing is the largest single sector in the area; it grew by 43 percent between 1964 and 1971, while the agricultural sector declined from 11 percent of the work force to 7 percent. A number of very large manufacturing plants cluster around Kngsport and Bristol, which, together with Elizabethton and Johnson City, account for over half of the area's industrial growth. The largest firms are found in chemicals (which employs one-third of the region's manufacturing workers but is hampered by lack of water resources), electronics, and paper and printing. Electrical machinery parts assembly, glass products, textiles and apparel plants add to employment opportunities.

At this writing, national economic recession has had a marked effect in the First Tennessee planning region. In October 1973 the unemployment rate was only 2.5 percent; in December 1974 it had risen to 9.5 percent. Manufacturing employment—especially in apparel, chemicals, electronics, and wood and wood products—has experienced abrupt reversals. The total work force dropped from 103,040 in October 1973 to 97,034 in December 1974. The outlook is for a slow upswing in the economy, with present employers calling back workers as national economic adjustments are made.

In establishing the First District's manpower service needs for fiscal year 1976, the manpower planning subcouncil has noted that the unemployed population is largely composed of recently terminated semiskilled workers with past job histories oriented toward piece-rate work. Most of these workers will need an opportunity to increase their skills either through formal classroom study or by on-the-job training. In addition, it is estimated that at least 2700 young people will drop out of school in 1976.

Many dropouts find low-paying jobs with few opportunities for advancement; often these jobs are eliminated as mechanization occurs. Higher-paying industries are located in the larger urban areas of the district, where needed services are available. Low-paying activities tend to locate in rural areas and to hire a high proportion of females, many of whom are capable of doing more sophisticated work. Usually, though, they cannot or will not relocate to take advantage of other job opportunities. Public service jobs are being created under the relevant CETA provisions, but the absence of construction funds for water and sewer projects, hospitals, schools and other public projects has retarded potential public service job development.

In view of the local manpower situation, the subcouncil's first priority for all CETA programs will be given to economically disadvantaged youth who are in school and who need financial assistance to complete their studies. Second priority will be given to unemployed persons who are not receiving unemployment insurance benefits and who have a potential to complete training offered by local CETA programs. Third priority will be given to unemployed persons who have recently been laid off and are nearing the retirement age.

Occupational training in the health field will have first job priority because health occupations are those projected to be in greatest demand over the remainder of the decade. Training in technical fields leading to skill level employment will also be stressed; these fields generally require more than 12 months of study. Second priority will be given to occupations for which the training period is less than 12 months. Public service employment will be developed in areas where community services are generally deficient—e.g., law enforcement, recreation, rural fire protection and rural health care.

First Tennessee manpower planners make some use of an employment service job bank to match workers and jobs within the district; they also can tie into the Knoxville labor market (and even into the rest of the state, which is rarely done). The main problem here is that employers very often do not list openings with the employment service, or at least not good jobs. Moreover, manpower training and services are geared to projected district needs and not to opportunities elsewhere.

First Tennessee has been able to identify and come to grips relatively effectively with local manpower problems for the same reasons found in the UCDD. There has been excellent leadership in both the development district and the manpower planning subcouncil. The district human resource agency has brought unity and efficiency to manpower service delivery. The agency has been effective because it has had the complete support of the district—i.e., the mayors and, even more important, the county judges who select the subcouncil chairman. Past experience has shown that political appointees do not make good manpower program administrators. To overcome this problem, three subcouncil members nominate three persons to fill any high level human resource agency opening. The agency head then selects one of the three for the job. It also should be noted the enactment of CETA gave the impetus to the creation of the human resource agency by local judges. Manpower planning under CETA, the subcouncil and the human resource agency is coordinated with development district planning through the A–95 review process. The locus for this coordination is one person who serves simultaneously as the district manpower representative, the state's manpower representative in the district and the CETA operations director.

In brief, then, although CETA does not represent a panacea for the vast range of manpower problems in nonmetropolitan areas,Tennessee experience indicates that with the cooperation of federal and state governments, local planning can, given strong leadership and a spirit of cooperation among local elected officials, be effective in formulating and implementing integrated area development and manpower service programs.

NOTES

[1] *The Comprehensive Employment and Training Act: Opportunities and Challenges* (Washington, D.C.: National Manpower Policy Task Force, April, 1974), p. 1.

[2] For examples, see *Area Development Interchange* 4, 1 (January 1, 1974): 3.

[3] Louis Levine, "Implications of CETA for Manpower Services in Rural Areas" (Paper presented at the CETA in Balance-of-State Areas Workshop, Washington, D.C., June 6-7, 1974), p. 7.

[4] Ibid., p. 8.

[5] Ibid., p. 11.

[6] Gerald Kraft et al., "On the Definition of a Depressed Area," in John F. Kain and John R. Meyer, *Essays in Regional Economics* (Cambridge: Harvard University Press, 1971), pp. 58–104.

[7] *Upper Cumberland Sub-council Area Manpower Plan, Fiscal Year 1975*, p. 3.

Chapter Seven

Access to Work Places

Knowledge of commuting behavior is essential to understanding the operation of functional labor market areas. Although many planners once believed that families would—or should—attempt to minimize the distance between home and work place, there is abundant evidence that both metropolitan and nonmetropolitan workers have been willing to commute over increasingly longer distances.

COMMUTING IN SMSAs

Anthony Catanese's analysis of commuting patterns in SMSAs indicates that while work trip minimization may be considered desirable by many families, it is not a discernible action as far as actual journey to work patterns are concerned. When deciding on a home location, an overwhelming majority of families have not regarded distance to work as an important factor.[1]

The relationship between family income and home-work separation is especially noteworthy. A priori it might be argued that families with high incomes are more likely to live close to their work places than would low income families, the reason being that they have a greater range of choice because of a lower cost constraint. In other words, high income families can afford higher housing costs and land rents near the central city where most of the relevant jobs are assumed to be located.

The alternative view is that:

[a]n individual's demand for a quality living environment appears to be income elastic. Therefore, the higher an individual's income, the more likely he is to choose a residential location which provides greater space and an attractive neighborhood. For numerous reasons the quality of living environments tends to increase farther from the location of business activity. This

is partly because business operations impose costs on the immediate neighborhood environment. Another reason is the tendency observed . . . of all major industry groups to be highly concentrated at the core of the city. Perhaps because of this and the lower intensity of land use and the lower average age of structures as one moves away from the central core, the residential environment is likely to improve as one moves out toward the suburban ring. It is therefore expected that in general employees in managerial, professional-technical and other high-paying occupations will commute farther due to both their larger normal preference areas and the fact that their expected level of residential amenities is likely to be met farther from the place of business activity.[2]

In fact, higher incomes generally are associated with longer trips to work in SMSAs. Low income families appear to be trapped in central cities and must commute largely away from the center to work places, which have been following middle and high income families to the suburbs. Curiously, the longer work trips of more affluent suburban residents are almost evenly divided between central city and suburban work places— i.e., although homes and jobs are decentralizing they are not decentralizing together to the same localities.[3] Continuing expansion of the suburbs would seem to imply that work trips will become longer. However, a word of caution is in order. Demographic projections are among the riskier ventures in the social sciences, and attempts to predict future commuting behavior on the basis of past tendencies may prove to be no better than similar efforts with respect to fertility and migration patterns. Moreover, while there is uncertainty concerning the elasticity of demand for gasoline in price ranges that have not been experienced heretofore in the United States, the energy situation certainly will work to reduce distances between residences and work places. Because of the compactness and density of SMSAs, adjustments to increase access to work places from homes may be easier than in nonmetropolitan areas.

COMMUTING IN NONMETROPOLITAN AREAS

Commuting by Rural Workers
In Chapter One it was shown that economic welfare in nonmetropolitan areas tends to be associated directly with ability to commute to an SMSA. Data presented in Chapter Two indicated that recent net outmigration from SMSAs to nonmetropolitan areas may be accounted for in part by the fact that increasingly people have been able to commute from SMSA fringe residences to jobs that have decentralized from central cities to suburbs and fringe areas of SMSAs. In addition, though, recent employment growth rates in nonmetropolitan areas have exceeded those in SMSAs, and recent population growth rates in counties not adjacent to SMSAs have

been higher than those in SMSAs. Adequate understanding of these phenomena requires express consideration of the role that commuting plays in providing rural workers access to employment opportunities.

Rural industries frequently draw their labor forces from remarkably wide geographic areas. Given an opportunity to work in an industrial plant, rural and small town residents have shown a marked tendency to maintain their established home and a willingness to commute great distances to work.[4] Moreover, residents of the open country and rural towns depend more on commuting for their employment than do people in small cities. In 1970 the proportion of these workers who commuted to work in another county was 24 percent. The comparable rate for residents in places of 2500 to 9999 population was 16 percent; and for residents in nonsuburban cities of 10,000 to 49,9999 population it was 11 percent.[5]

> Commuting has permitted the population in many rural locations to stabilize or even continue to increase regardless of local job conditions. Much commuting is to nonmetro cities of 10,000 to 49,999 population. Those communities are the most self-contained in our entire settlement network. Their residents are far less likely to engage in intercounty job commuting than are residents of any other type of settlement—less likely even than metro central-city people on one hand and farmers on the other.[6]

Small Towns and Outsized Functions

The role of commuting in maintaining populations in many rural areas is not only a matter of linking home and factory. It also plays an important part in the preservation of businesses which continue to exist and even thrive despite general local economic decline. Central place studies usually show that the variety of goods and services provided by a place is closely correlated with its population size. Thus most small towns come off rather poorly when judged in terms of central place functions. Yet many small towns have at least one firm that has prospered in relation to other local activities. The term "outsized function" has been used to describe this phenomenon because qualitatively it seems out of place in its local setting. It has been argued that just as a city dweller may spend a fair portion of his day traveling from one localized functional area to another, so a farmer or small town resident may drive to many small towns to obtain the goods and services provided by their outsized functions. A man who lives in town A, for example, may work in town B and on Saturday buy groceries in town C, go to the area's best hardware store in town D, look over an automobile in town E and stop off at a tavern in town F on the way home.[7]

Unfortunately, this view of a rural area as a kind of dispersed city in terms of shopping has serious limitations. It is based on observations from what are, in a rural context, relatively densely settled and prosperous

Middle Western areas. It also assumes the ubiquitous ownership of automobiles and plentiful, cheap gasoline. The SMSA resident who feels the pinch of the energy crunch can at least do most or all of his shopping at a single large shopping mall. His country cousin will not have this option unless he drives what may be a considerable distance to a large city. But then what becomes of the outsized functions in the rural area?

Transportation in Rural Areas

Even more to the point is the fact that in most rural areas a large proportion of the population is deprived or handicapped with respect to automobile transportation. The data in Table 7–1 show, by state, the proportion of rural nonfarm and farm households in each of these categories. The data were compiled from a random sample of the noncommuter and commuter rural counties shown on Map 1–1. The rationale for the breakdown in Table 7–1 is that "In most rural counties a household without any automobile is *deprived* of transportation. Since, as we have seen, the private automobile is used extensively by the breadwinner of the household to commute to and from work, it is fair to assume that a rural household with only one automobile is transportation *handicapped*. In any rural area the handicapped will include the deprived."[8] The extent of the rural transportation problem is indicated by the fact that the rural area of Colorado had the lowest proportion of households of any state in the handicapped category, yet even here 52.8 percent were so classified. There are 12 states where over 20 percent of all households are deprived; conversely, only four states have less than 10 percent of their households in the deprived category. In 28 states, over two-thirds of the relevant households are transportation handicapped.

Commuting, Migration and Long Run Stability

Finally, even where there is a great deal of commuting in rural areas it is not certain that this will stabilize the size of the local population. Despite the need for much more thorough research, there is some evidence that strong linkages exist between external commuting and outmigration.[9] However, external commuting, unlike migration, can be a means for capitalizing on private and community investment in areas experiencing employment decline or stagnation. But such commuting is therefore highly dependent on the availability of these residual assets at low prices to compensate for the cost of long daily journeys to work. And such communities, unless they are absorbed by the spread of metropolitan areas, are not likely to be durable in the long run. "Demographic decline is guaranteed through the persistent failure of young entrants to the commuting workforce to replace the wastage of established commuters through re-

Table 7-1.   Transportation Status of Households in Rural Counties, 1970

	Total		Rural Nonfarm		Farm Occupied	
	Deprived	Handi-capped	Deprived	Handi-capped	Deprived	Handi-capped
Alabama	20.7	62.8	25.4	71.9	14.5	61.6
Arizona	20.0	66.3	21.9	68.0	27.0	75.1
Arkansas	25.8	76.8	24.0	76.7	21.8	76.7
California	11.0	64.7	9.7	63.3	9.1	66.6
Colorado	10.9	52.8	11.1	64.6	4.9	66.2
Florida	19.3	72.2	17.9	71.6	12.0	60.9
Georgia	20.8	68.4	19.3	68.7	8.7	61.6
Idaho	10.1	60.6	7.8	59.1	4.4	52.8
Illinois	13.6	73.1	11.6	73.2	6.3	74.8
Indiana	13.0	69.4	9.8	68.5	5.8	68.0
Iowa	12.1	69.2	9.9	69.7	3.0	69.1
Kansas	11.8	69.4	7.9	67.9	4.4	69.1
Kentucky	26.5	77.2	26.5	78.1	15.5	74.6
Louisiana	24.7	72.6	22.2	72.5	13.1	62.9
Maine	14.8	74.2	14.3	73.5	12.8	80.1
Maryland	16.6	70.1	14.4	68.1	9.3	66.8
Massachusetts	14.9	67.2	10.8	67.1	4.8	53.1
Michigan	9.9	67.5	9.0	67.4	*	*
Minnesota	10.1	64.3	8.3	64.3	3.1	63.7
Mississippi	27.4	75.1	26.6	77.0	22.3	74.7
Missouri	20.2	76.7	18.2	76.0	7.2	74.0
Montana	13.6	58.1	13.2	53.2	7.7	62.6
Nebraska	10.3	68.1	8.6	67.6	2.6	65.5
New Hampshire	10.7	59.8	8.0	53.7	1.5	57.1
New Mexico	19.1	71.8	21.0	74.8	15.8	64.0
New York	14.7	72.9	11.2	70.3	5.3	62.5
North Carolina	21.2	66.1	20.1	67.4	17.6	66.0
North Dakota	9.9	70.9	8.6	75.1	2.0	69.5
Ohio	12.8	65.3	10.8	64.0	6.0	62.9
Oklahoma	17.7	73.9	16.8	75.1	11.2	67.7
Oregon	10.3	60.0	7.9	58.0	4.0	55.2
Pennsylvania	11.9	65.8	10.8	64.9	8.0	62.6
South Carolina	24.6	71.5	24.4	73.6	18.8	73.7
South Dakota	10.1	66.6	8.3	69.0	2.7	66.0
Tennessee	20.6	68.8	20.4	69.4	17.2	67.2
Texas	1.5	67.2	15.0	72.0	7.0	67.6
Utah	8.5	58.6	9.0	63.5	6.0	63.1
Vermont	14.0	74.8	12.6	73.9	4.8	62.6
Virginia	19.2	69.6	19.2	69.9	16.8	69.7
Washington	11.3	64.2	8.8	64.4	3.6	61.2
West Virginia	20.9	74.1	20.7	73.6	15.1	69.7
Wisconsin	11.9	68.9	9.9	67.6	3.8	64.6
Wyoming	10.3	65.0	9.1	65.5	7.4	67.2

Source: *The Transportation of People in Rural Areas,* Committee Print prepared for the Subcommittee on Rural Development, Committee on Agriculture and Forestry, U.S. Senate, 93rd Cong., 2nd sess., February 27, 1974 (Washington, D.C.: Government Printing Office, 1974), p. 3.

*Not available

tirement and outmigration. Residential decline is assured by low housing values, minimal maintenance, and lack of new construction."[10] This is not to say that external commuting under such conditions is without value. Clearly it is an important means of adjustment and it transfers enough of the prosperity of the workplace back to the source area to sustain the latter's residential role in the short run. Then, too, there is always the chance that spontaneous economic changes will result in a revival of local employment opportunities. In the absence of such good fortune, John Holmes maintains that:

> External commuting possibly represents a permanent or durable condition only for the open-country population on residential or parttime farms. This type of commuting does not necessarily originate in a stranded population, nor is it dependent upon such ephemeral assets as cheap housing. The durable qualities of open-country living will continue to appeal to an important sector of the population.[11]

In the context of the United States this finding has somewhat elitist implications. It suggests that areas experiencing outmigration and external commuting will eventually be inhabited by a few relatively wealthy farm owners and from time to time by city dwellers with the means to maintain second homes in pleasant rural areas. This may turn out to be the case; rising per capita real incomes may also eventually bring these opportunities within reach of "an important sector of the population," assuming that Holmes is referring to numbers rather than status. However, with the exception of regions well endowed with mountains, lakes, and similar natural (and manmade) amenities, the outcome he describes will probably not be typical.

For example, about 1350 counties—well over a third of all those in the nation—had such heavy outmigration during the 1960s that they experienced absolute population declines. (About 500 counties had fewer births than deaths in 1970 because so many young adults had left; in 1960 there were only 38 such counties and in 1950 only two!) These counties are overwhelmingly rural in nature and are concentrated in several large multistate regions. External commuting is limited by a number of factors in these regions. In central Appalachia commuting is restricted by mountainous terrain and poor roads, which pose particular problems in the winter. In an even larger block of counties experiencing population decline—that extending from the southern Atlantic Coastal Plains across through central Georgia, Alabama and Mississippi into southeastern Arkansas and northeastern Louisiana—commuting is sharply restricted because there are few industrial jobs; and the blacks, who represent a high proportion of the total population, usually lack adequate transportation means. By far the largest block of declining counties extends along the Canadian border from Montana to Minnesota and southward through the Great Plains and the Corn Belt to the Texas-Mexican border. Sparse populations spread over great distances and lack of industrialization have precluded significant amounts of commuting to work in most of this area, though there are exceptions in the Corn Belt.

In Chapter Two it was pointed out that the largest block of counties in the nation that reversed population decline and grew in the 1960s was located in the Ozarks regions. It also was shown that improved population retention has not removed a host of problems with respect to poverty, human resource development and employment opportunities. In contrast, outmigration from the Great Plains and the Corn Belt has consisted for the most part of retired farmers moving to warmer climates and young people well prepared to take advantage of economic opportunities in other areas. There is relatively little poverty among the people left behind (though access to services is often a problem) and agriculture is viable and will no doubt become even more remunerative given the rapid increase in world demand for food.

In sum, then, while migration and external commuting may be directly related in some areas, and while they may in some instances cushion short run adaptations to long run, and perhaps desirable, adjustments, these processes are by no means accurate reflections of what is happening in large segments of nonmetropolitan society in the United States—even where net outmigration is substantial.

SIMULATING GREATER SCALE IN NONMETROPOLITAN AREAS

While commuting may be an adaptation to decline, it may also represent an opportunity for promoting the viability of nonmetropolitan areas. Thus, a group of small centers might attempt to simulate greater scale. Wilbur Thompson has remarked that:

> A number of small- and medium-size urban areas, connected by good highways and/or rail lines may form a loose network of interrelated labor markets. With widespread ownership of automobiles and a well-developed bus system on expressways permitting average speeds of 50 miles an hour, the effective local labor market would extend radially for 25 to 30 miles around one of the larger urban places. A couple of small cities of, say, 25,000 population, with two or three main industries each, plus a half dozen one- or two-industry towns of half that size add up to a 100,000 to 200,000 population, extended local labor market, built on the moderately broad base of more than a dozen important industries.

The case for the federated local labor market can be made more programmatically by promoting a comprehensive and coordinated employment service. The local labor market could then achieve the scale necessary to offer the counseling and teaching so critical in our rapidly changing economy.[12]

Thompson further argues that:

In such complexes, both public and private investments could be planned strategically. Instead of many small, bare community halls sprinkled across the area, one spacious, acoustically pleasing auditorium could be built. In place of a couple of two-year community colleges staffed as extensions of the local high schools, a strong four-year college could be supported. Nearby and inexpensive higher education—commuter colleges—may be critical in holding in the area talented young from middle- and low-income homes, and perhaps in attracting those families in the first place. Again museums, professional athletic teams, complete medical facilities, and other accoutrements of modern urban life could be supported collectively. The smaller urban places could become analogous to the dormitory suburbs of the large metropolitan area, with their central business districts serving as regional shopping centers. The largest or most centrally located town could become the central business district—downtown—for the whole network of urban places, with travel times not significantly greater than those which now exist in the typical million population metropolitan areas. As these federated places grew and prospered, the interstices would, of course, begin to fill in, moving the area closer to the large metropolitan area form. But alert action in land planning and zoning could preserve open spaces in a pattern superior to those found in most large urban areas.[13]

In Thompson's view, North Carolina—a state with numerous small and medium-size cities—would be a logical place to implement these proposals. The Piedmont Crescent of North Carolina does in fact provide a remarkable example of decentralized urbanization. However, in 1970 this area had four SMSAs: Raleigh, Durham, Greensboro–Winston-Salem–High Point and Charlotte. Therefore it is not appropriate to consider the Piedmont Crescent in the present nonmetropolitan context.

NONMETROPOLITAN REGIONS AS FUNCTIONAL LABOR MARKETS

Study Regions Defined

Nevertheless, there are many nonmetropolitan areas where large numbers of people live within reasonable commuting range of one another and where the application of projects and programs along the lines suggested by Thompson merits serious consideration. I selected a set of such regions on the basis of detailed map studies. There were three basic criteria for selection. First, the counties involved should be beyond normal commuting distance to an SMSA. Second, people within the region should, for the most part, be within commuting distance of one another. Third, the counties in the region should have a total population of at least 100,000 persons, the threshold level for Thompson's federated multicounty labor markets. Also, for an area to be a prime sponsor of manpower programs under the Comprehensive Employment and Training Act of 1973 it must have a minimum population of 100,000 persons. This does not mean that a group of nonmetropolitan counties with more than 100,000 persons can actually qualify as a prime sponsor. The problem is that such areas do not have any unit of government to act as a prime sponsor; thus, prime sponsors are normally in metropolitan areas and the nonmetropolitan areas fall into a "balance-of-state" category and are the responsibility of the various governors. In other words, if the 100,000 figure does represent a kind of rough indicator of labor market viability—and this may be disputed both by those who would argue that it is too high and those taking a contrary position—there is an economic if not a juridical basis for the regions selected.

As a check on the accuracy of the nonmetropolitan regions selected, state rural manpower officials were contacted. They were shown the counties selected and the criteria for selection and were asked to comment on the appropriateness of the choices. As a consequence of this review some regions were dropped from further consideration; in some other cases counties were added or dropped to obtain the final set of 49 regions shown in Appendix A.

The following sections present data on workers' use of public transportation and on commuting in these nonmetropolitan regions. Data on income and poverty status also are presented. Comparisons are made with corresponding data from relatively nearby SMSAs (see Appendix B) and with a set of 20 urban regions characterized by the kind of decentralized urbanization already discussed in relation to North Carolina (see Appendix C).

Public Transportation and Welfare Indicators

Ira Kaye states that:

> The place that the mobility needs of the people has in the thought processes of our planners is best indicated by the recently published "Social Indicators 1973," written and compiled by the Statistical Policy Division, Office of Management and Budget.

> Amidst the wealth of charts and tables, only one is devoted to mobility and it reflects only the use of the private automobile and/or public transportation as a means of getting to work. Although almost all of the 1970 data in the table is listed as "Not Available," what does stand out, comparing 1963 to 1970, is that the percentage of those using the private automobile to get to work has

risen from 82% to 87% while the percentage of those using public transportation declined from 14% to 10%.

None of this data is broken down to enable us to compare the rural population's mode of travel with that of our urbanites.[14]

The cross-sectional data presented and analyzed in the remainder of this chapter represent a partial attempt to fill in gaps in knowledge with respect to how journey to work differences are related to place of residence.

The proportion of workers using public transportation in their journey to work is shown in Table 7–2 by type of region: nonmetropolitan, SMSA or dispersed urban. Moreover, within each of these categories there is a South–non-South breakdown. The South includes all the states of the Confederacy with the addition of Kentucky and West Virginia, but excluding west Texas. Table 7–2 also gives weighted and unweighted averages; the tests of statistical significance results presented in Table 7–3 (and similar subsequent tables) are based on the unweighted means, which in this case are shown in parentheses in Table 7–2.

Looking first at the weighted means, the data clearly indicate that workers in the nonmetropolitan regions do not use public transportation to work to the same extent as workers in SMSAs or dispersed urban regions. The 5.92 percent value for SMSAs is over four times the corresponding nonmetropolitan value; the 3.30 percent value for dispersed urban areas is well over twice that of the nonmetropolitan value. The unweighted differences are not quite as great, but they are still highly significant at the 0.01 level (see Table 7–3). The relative lack of use of public transportation by nonmetropolitan workers is not simply a matter of taste; all aspects of the research for this study made it abundantly evident that nonmetropolitan areas are highly disadvantaged with respect to access to economic opportunities made possible by public transportation facilities.

Although the proportion of workers in the South using public transportation in their journey to work is greater than that for non-South workers (the difference is significant at the 0.01 level), it is still very small, both absolutely and in relation to South and non-South workers in SMSAs and in dispersed urban areas. As might be expected, the mean values for workers in dispersed urban regions fall in between those for nonmetropolitan regions on the one hand and SMSAs on the other.

Table 7–2 also presents data on two key welfare indicators: median family income and percent of the total population in poverty. Tests of significance of differences in median family income are shown in Table 7–4; corresponding tests for mean proportion of the population in poverty are shown in Table 7–5. The weighted median family income figure of $7933 for nonmetropolitan regions is well below the corresponding $9832 for SMSAs and $9083 for dispersed urban regions. The difference between the unweighted nonmetropolitan median family income value and those for both

Table 7–2. Workers Using Public Transportation, Median Family Income, and Poverty Incidence in Selected Counties, Mean Values, 1970

	Nonmetropolitan Regions[1]			SMSAs[1]			Dispersed Urban Regions[1]		
	Total	South	Non-South	Total	South	Non-South	Total	South	Non-South
Percent of workers using public transportation to work	1.44 (1.35)[2]	1.92 (1.80)	1.04 (1.02)	5.92 (3.97)	7.79 (4.92)	4.79 (3.26)	3.30 (2.91)	3.80 (3.67)	2.83 (2.51)
Median family income (dollars)	7,933 (7,909)	7,121 (7,007)	8,631 (8,586)	9,832 (9,314)	8,841 (8,374)	10,443 (10,011)	9,083 (8,998)	8,404 (8,301)	9,505 (9,373)
Percent of population in poverty	17.4 (17.4)	23.0 (23.3)	12.7 (12.9)	12.2 (13.2)	17.1 (17.9)	9.2 (9.8)	14.1 (15.4)	17.6 (18.0)	12.5 (13.9)

Source: U.S. Bureau of the Census, *County and City Data Book, 1972* (Washington, D.C.: Government Printing Office, 1973).

[1] For details concerning the counties included, see Appendixes A, B and C.

[2] Values in parentheses are unweighted means.

Table 7–3. *T*-Values for Tests of Significance of Differences in Mean Percent of Workers Using Public Transportation to Work During Census Week, 1970

	Nonmetro-politan Non-South	SMSA South	SMSA Non-South	Dispersed Urban Region South	Dispersed Urban Region Non-South
Nonmetropolitan South	−3.44*	3.15*	2.85*	4.73*	1.91
Nonmetropolitan Non-South		4.58*	5.09*	8.48*	4.87*
SMSA South			−1.67	−0.73	−1.89
SMSA Non-South				0.46	−1.14
Dispersed urban region South					−2.10**

	All SMSAs	All Dispersed Urban Regions
All nonmetro-politan regions	5.19*	5.88*
All SMSAs		−0.133

Source: My computations from U.S. Bureau of the Census, *County and City Data Book 1972* (Washington, D.C.: U.S. Government Printing Office, 1973).
*Significant at the 0.01 level
**Significant at the 0.05 level

SMSAs and dispersed urban regions is significant at the 0.01 level (See Table 7–4).

It is noteworthy that the nonmetropolitan regions outside the South have median family incomes significantly *below* non-South SMSAs and non-South dispersed urban regions. Yet they are significantly *above* median family incomes in the nonmetropolitan regions of the South and not significantly different from Southern SMSAs and dispersed urban regions. Within the South, SMSA and dispersed urban region median incomes are not significantly different, but both have significantly higher median income levels than nonmetropolitan regions. Non-South SMSAs have higher median incomes than any other type of area and—with the exception of non-South dispersed urban regions—the difference is significant at the 0.01 level in each case.

Geographic differences in incidence of poverty are similar to those for median family income. The highest rates of poverty are found in the nonmetropolitan regions, and particularly in the South, where nearly a quarter of the population was in poverty in 1970. The incidence of poverty in dispersed urban regions was lower than in nonmetropolitan regions but

Table 7.-4. *T*-Values for Tests of Significance of Differences in Mean Median Family Income, 1970

	Nonmetro- politan Non-South	SMSA South	SMSA Non- South	Dispersed Urban Region South	Dispersed Urban Region Non-South
Nonmetropolitan South	6.19*	4.97*	12.34*	3.65*	5.47*
Nonmetropolitan Non-South		−0.83	6.34*	−0.83	2.02**
SMSA South			6.75*	−0.21	2.30**
SMSA Non-South				−5.47*	−1.68
Dispersed urban region South					1.68

	All SMSAs	All Dispersed Urban Regions
All nonmetropolitan regions	5.90*	3.28*
All SMSAs		−0.96

Source: My computations from data in U.S. Bureau of the Census, *County and City Data Book 1972* (Washington, D.C.: U.S. Government Printing Office, 1973).

*Significant at the 0.01 level
**Significant at the 0.05 level

higher than in SMSAs. However, there was a considerable difference between South and non-South SMSAs. The latter had the lowest poverty rate—less than 10 percent. Poverty incidence in Southern SMSAs was not only significantly greater than in non-South SMSAs, but also significantly greater than in nonmetropolitan regions outside the South. Indeed, it is striking that the incidence of poverty in nonmetropolitan regions outside the South is significantly lower than in any category of Southern area—nonmetropolitan, SMSA or dispersed urban.

If the data in Table 7–2 were not disaggregated regionally, it would appear that access to employment opportunities as reflected in the proportion of workers using public transportation to work is directly related to median family income and inversely related to poverty incidence. Disaggregation reveals a different picture. For example, the use by Southern nonmetropolitan workers of public transportation to work is significantly greater than the corresponding value for nonmetropolitan non-South workers, yet Southern nonmetropolitan workers are in a significantly worse position with respect to each of the welfare indicators. Similar patterns exist within SMSAs and dispersed urban regions: Southern workers make greater use of public transportation to work but they have lower welfare indicators than their non-South counterparts.

Table 7-5. T-Values for Tests of Significance of Differences in Mean Percent of Total Population in Poverty, 1970

	Nonmetro- politan Non-South	SMSA South	SMSA Non- South	Dispersed Urban Region South	Dispersed Urban Region Non-South
Nonmetropolitan South	−6.36*	−2.92*	−9.18*	−1.82	−2.98*
Nonmetropolitan Non-South		4.58*	−4.10*	3.27*	0.44
SMSA South			−10.50*	0.04	−1.52
SMSA Non-South				10.10*	1.97**
Dispersed urban region South					−0.95

	All SMSAs	All Dispersed Urban Regions
All nonmetropolitan regions	−3.16*	−0.95
All SMSAs		1.24

Source: My computations from data in U.S. Bureau of the Census, *County and City Data Book 1972* (Washington, D.C.: U.S. Government Printing Office, 1973).

*Significant at the 0.01 level
**Significant at the 0.05 level

In this context it is instructive to examine the SMSA data more carefully and to consider a case study of the Atlanta SMSA. Looking only at SMSAs, median family income is significantly lower in the South and poverty incidence is significantly higher. In terms of unweighted means, the proportion of Southern workers using public transportation is 4.92 percent; the corresponding non-South value is 3.26 percent. Although this difference is substantial, it is not significant at the 0.05 level. However, the weighted mean value for the South is 7.79 percent, while that for the non-South is 4.79 percent; this difference is greater in both absolute and percentage terms than the difference in the unweighted means. Obviously one cannot conclude on this basis that use of public transportation in the journey to work is inversely related to welfare. Income levels and poverty are influenced by a host of complex and interrelated factors in addition to availability and use of public transportation. On the other hand, these results lend support to findings derived from a careful study of job accessibility and underemployment in the Atlanta SMSA.

Mass transit advocates in Atlanta have argued that improved accessibility between job centers and low income neighborhoods would help alleviate the underemployment problems of inner city workers. Bederman and Adams tested the hypothesis that census tracts with high rates of underemployment should be those with low accessibility to jobs.[15] They found that tracts at every accessibility level showed a wide range in percentages of underemployment and tracts with high job accessibility failed to show low underemployment. Indeed, the simple correlation between percent underemployed and average accessibility score for 37 sample tracts was +0.55—i.e., the closer the jobs the higher was the underemployment rate. After examining other variables that might account for the distribution of underemployment within the tracts at each accessibility level, it was found that improved public transportation facilities might increase the comfort and convenience of unskilled workers, but it would not substantially affect their economic condition.

> In Atlanta, the distribution of underemployment, measured by income below the poverty line or less than full-time employment, is better explained by skill levels, discrimination, and socioeconomic circumstance than by accessibility to jobs. At every level of accessibility underemployment is worst among female heads of families, mostly black, poorly educated, with several children. Underemployment could better be tackled through job training, placement, and child care programs than through new transit development programs.[16]

The results of one case study of Atlanta do not in themselves justify generalizations about the United States or even the South. However, they are consistent with evidence presented in earlier chapters with respect to human resource development deficiencies in rural areas throughout the nation, and particularly in the South. Moreover, disadvantaged persons in rural areas do not enjoy the potential accessibility to jobs that apparently exists in Atlanta. Distances from residences to potential work places obviously are much greater and public transportation means usually are lacking. Thus, the fact that the proportion of nonmetropolitan Southern workers who use public transportation to work is significantly greater than the corresponding non-South proportion is rather trivial. In both cases the proportion is less than 2 percent.

Commuting

Although they lack public transportation facilities, the data in Table 7–6 clearly indicate that many nonmetropolitan workers are willing to commute to work.[17] A commuter is defined to be a person who works in a county other than his county of residence. In 1970, over 13 percent of the workers in the reporting work force of the nonmetropolitan regions commuted to work. The figure was somewhat higher in the South, but not significantly greater than in the non-South regions (see Table 7–7). It is especially noteworthy that the proportion of commuters in the nonmet-

Table 7-6.   Commuting Data (Mean Values) for Selected Counties, 1970

	Nonmetropolitan Regions[1]			SMSAs[1]			Dispersed Urban Regions[1]		
	Total	South	Non-South	Total	South	Non-South	Total	South	Non-South
Commuters as percent of total reporting work force	13.43 (13.14)[2]	14.41 (14.18)	12.62 (12.36)	17.38 (13.27)	19.81 (15.21)	15.93 (11.84)	12.66 (11.63)	14.02 (14.05)	11.32 (10.32)
Percent of total work force commuting out of region	5.53 (5.53)	5.25 (5.48)	5.75 (5.57)	2.23 (2.73)	1.97 (2.55)	2.39 (2.86)	2.01 (2.01)	1.53 (1.67)	2.38 (2.19)
Outcommuters as percent of all commuters	41.13 (39.76)	36.45 (39.75)	45.58 (39.78)	12.84 (30.11)	9.96 (26.09)	14.97 (33.09)	15.91 (18.54)	10.88 (12.39)	21.07 (21.86)

Source: Compiled from data supplied by Bureau of Economic Analysis, U.S. Department of Commerce.

1. For details concerning the counties included, see Appendixes A, B and C.

2. Values in parentheses are unweighted means.

ropolitan regions was not significantly different from that in SMSAs or dispersed urban regions. Among the comparisons shown in Table 7–7, the only significant difference was that between the nonmetropolitan South and non-South dispersed urban regions, which had the lowest rate of any group—10.3 percent.

In the nonmetropolitan regions, 5.53 percent of the reporting work force commuted to work places outside the regions. About two out of every five commuters went outside the regions' counties. Measured either way, commuting out of region was significantly higher in nonmetropolitan regions than in both SMSAs and dispersed urban regions (see Tables 7-8 and 7–9). There was no significant difference between nonmetropolitan regions in the South and in the non-South areas. There also was no significant difference in proportion of the total work force commuting out of region between SMSAs and dispersed urban regions; however, outcommuters as a proportion of all commuters was significantly greater in SMSAs than in dispersed urban regions.

In general, these results reflect the more geographically dispersed nature of employment opportunities in nonmetropolitan areas, but also the willingness of many workers to overcome lack of direct access by commuting.

Table 7–7. *T*-Values for Tests of Significance of Differences in Mean Percent of Commuters as Percent of Total Reporting Work Force, 1970

	Nonmetro-politan Non-South	*SMSA South*	*SMSA Non-South*	*Dispersed Urban Region South*	*Dispersed Urban Region Non-South*
Nonmetropolitan South	−1.17	0.41	−1.24	−0.06	−2.17**
Nonmetropolitan Non-South		1.25	−0.30	0.78	−1.16
SMSA South			−1.32	−0.29	−1.62
SMSA Non-South				0.78	−0.68
Dispersed urban region South					−1.90

	All SMSAs	*All Dispersed Urban Regions*
All nonmetropolitan regions	0.09	−1.10
All SMSAs		−0.80

Source: My computations from data from source on Table 7–6.
**Significant at the 0.05 level

Table 7–8. *T*-Values for Tests of Significance of Differences in Mean Percent of Total Work Force Commuting Out of Region, 1970

	Nonmetro-politan Non-South	SMSA South	SMSA Non-South	Dispersed Urban Region South	Dispersed Urban Region Non-South
Nonmetropolitan South	0.085	−5.02*	−3.68*	−4.28*	−4.79*
Nonmetropolitan Non-South		−2.85*	−2.69*	−2.21**	−2.60**
SMSA South			0.49	−1.75	−0.84
SMSA Non-South				−1.20	−0.90
Dispersed urban region South					1.10

	All SMSAs	All Dispersed Urban Regions
All nonmetro-politan regions	−4.49*	−4.12*
All SMSAs		−1.46

Source: My computations from data from source on Table 7–6.
 *Significant at the 0.01 level
**Significant at the 0.05 level

Tables 7–10 through 7–13 report the results of regressions that were calculated in an attempt to gain greater insight into relationships between commuting and independent variables that were believed to be associated with different levels of commuting. The variables used are as follows:

PERWF	Commuters as percent of total reporting work force, 1970.
PEROUT	Percent of total work force commuting to places outside of region.
OUTPWF	Persons who commuted outside of region as a percent of all commuters.
AREA	Total square miles in region.
POPDEN	Population density in number of persons per square mile.
BLACK	Blacks as a percent of total population, 1970.
MANUF	Percent of civilian labor force employed in manufacturing, 1970.
PROFMAN	Percent of civilian labor force employed in professional and managerial categories.

Table 7-9. *T*-Values for Tests of Significance of Differences in Mean Number of Outcommuters as a Percent of All Commuters, 1970

	Nonmetro-politan Non-South	SMSA South	SMSA Non-South	Dispersed Urban Region South	Dispersed Urban Region Non-South
Nonmetropolitan South	0.005	−2.45**	−1.04	−5.21*	−4.36*
Nonmetropolitan Non-South		−2.08**	−0.99	−3.07**	−2.70**
SMSA South			0.96	−1.66	−0.68
SMSA Non-South				−2.02	−1.48
Dispersed urban region South					2.97*

	All SMSAs	All Dispersed Urban Regions
All nonmetro-politan regions	−2.14**	−4.69*
All SMSAs		−2.05**

Source: My computations from data from source on Table 7-6.

*Significant at the 0.01 level

**Significant at the 0.05 level

PUBTRANS	Percent of workers using public transportation to work during census week, 1970.
REGION	A dummy variable; South = 1, non-South = 0.
MEDAGE	Median age of the population, 1970.

It was hypothesized that AREA would be inversely related to commuting, especially to commuting out of region. The smaller the residential area the easier it would be for workers to reach employment opportunities elsewhere. POPDEN was also hypothesized to be inversely related to commuting. If density of population is related to density of jobs, then more opportunities might be available in the worker's county of residence if it is relatively densely settled—i.e., he will not have as great a need to commute. Because blacks tend to be disadvantaged in so many respects—including transportation means—it was expected that commuting would be inversely related to BLACK. Evidence cited earlier in this chapter indicates considerable willingness on the part of many workers in nonmetropolitan areas to commute considerable distances to factory work. Thus, it was hypothesized that MANUF would be directly related to commuting.

Table 7–10. Regressions Relating Eight Independent Variables to Commuting Variables in Nonmetropolitan Regions, SMSAs and Dispersed Urban Areas

Independent Variables	Dependent Variables								
	Nonmetropolitan Regions			SMSAs			Dispersed Urban Areas		
	PERWF	PEROUT	OUTPWF	PERWF	PEROUT	OUTPWF	PERWF	PEROUT	OUTPWF
Constant	23.7	16.1	69.3	45.6	-3.32	-83.4	-0.211	-4.50	-18.0
AREA	-0.00050 (-1.14)	-0.00063* (-2.15)	-0.0034* (-2.32)	0.0013 (0.96)	-0.00032 (-0.84)	-0.0051 (-1.19)	-0.000084 (-0.38)	-0.000027 (-0.62)	-0.000038 (-0.082)
POPDEN	0.048 (1.78)	-0.0029 (-0.16)	-0.13 (-1.41)	0.0091 (0.84)	-0.0018 (-0.61)	-0.032 (-0.98)	-0.026 (-1.14)	0.00025 (0.056)	0.032 (0.68)
BLACK	-0.14 (-1.82)	0.035 (0.67)	0.53* (2.09)	0.026 (0.14)	0.043 (0.82)	-0.14 (-0.24)	-0.051 (-0.33)	-0.0041 (-0.13)	0.046 (0.14)
MANUF	-0.092 (-0.88)	-0.019 (-0.28)	0.15 (0.43)	-0.12 (-0.65)	0.087 (1.71)	0.64 (1.13)	0.34 (2.15)	0.033 (1.05)	-0.17 (-0.49)
PROFMAN	-0.55 (-1.30)	-0.70* (-2.51)	-3.35* (-2.42)	-0.99* (-2.27)	0.052 (0.44)	3.00* (2.27)	-0.011 (-0.034)	-0.0027 (-0.041)	0.12 (0.18)
PUBTRANS	0.71 (0.71)	0.64 (0.96)	3.25 (0.98)	0.33 (0.59)	-0.097 (-0.65)	-1.06 (-0.64)	0.33 (0.32)	-0.29 (-1.41)	-1.99 (-0.93)
REGION	2.02 (0.94)	-2.94* (-2.06)	-19.9** (-2.81)	1.33 (0.35)	-0.89 (-0.86)	-2.70 (-0.23)	3.01 (0.86)	-0.36 (-0.52)	-8.14 (-1.11)
MEDAGE	0.0075 (0.031)	0.21 (1.27)	1.74* (2.18)	-0.47 (-0.70)	0.14 (0.79)	1.81 (0.89)	0.24 (0.56)	0.26* (2.91)	1.54 (1.66)
R^2	0.384	0.425	0.475	0.285	0.245	0.310	0.622	0.699	0.488
R^2 adj.	0.261	0.310	0.370	0.130	0.082	0.160	0.348	0.480	0.116
F Test	3.11**	3.69**	4.52**	1.84	1.50	2.08	2.27	3.19*	1.31

Source: My computations from data given in U.S. Bureau of the Census, *County and City Data Book 1972.* Washington D.C.: U.S. Government Printing Office, 1973.

*Significant at the 0.05 level
**Significant at the 0.01 level
Values in parentheses are *t*-ratios.

Table 7-11. Regressions Relating Seven Independent Variables to Commuting Variables in Nonmetropolitan Regions

Independent Variables	Dependent Variables					
	South			Non-South		
	PERWF	PEROUT	OUTPWF	PERWF	PEROUT	OUTPWF
Constant	25.6	3.45	-28.1	46.1	24.4	73.7
AREA	-0.0041 (-1.72)	-0.0011 (-0.77)	0.0041 (0.56)	-0.00053 (-1.06)	-0.00052 (-1.51)	-0.0026 (-1.61)
POPDEN	0.012 (0.26)	-0.022 (-0.80)	-0.127 (-0.89)	0.056 (1.45)	0.042 (0.16)	-0.13 (-1.08)
BLACK	-0.18 (-1.95)	-0.024 (-0.44)	0.21 (0.74)	-0.21 (-0.53)	-0.022 (-0.080)	1.38 (1.06)
MANUF	0.079 (0.54)	0.072 (0.82)	0.28 (0.62)	-0.31 (-1.88)	-0.087 (-0.76)	0.35 (0.65)
PROFMAN	0.515 (0.78)	0.305 (0.77)	1.00 (0.49)	-1.37* (-2.32)	-1.19** (-2.91)	-4.28* (-2.25)
PUBTRANS	0.199 (0.12)	0.037 (0.038)	-0.57 (-0.11)	0.76 (0.54)	0.87 (0.90)	4.92 (1.90)
MEDAGE	-0.44 (-1.07)	-0.047 (-0.19)	1.38 (1.08)	-0.011 (-0.031)	0.28 (1.78)	1.88 (1.60)
R^2	0.552	0.142	0.341	0.435	0.614	.670
R^2 adj.	0.310	-0.321	-0.013	0.237	0.478	0.555
F Test	2.29	0.31	0.96	2.20	4.53**	5.82**

*Significant at the 0.05 level.
**Significant at the 0.01 level
Values in parentheses are t-ratios.

Table 7–12.   Regressions Relating Seven Independent Variables to Commuting Variables in SMSAs

| | Dependent Variables | | | | | |
| | *South* | | | *Non-South* | | |
Independent Variables	*PERWF*	*PEROUT*	*OUTPWF*	*PERWF*	*PEROUT*	*OUTPWF*
Constant	54.7	−5.21	−62.2	32.3	−3.79	−135.8
AREA	0.0059	−0.00056	−0.021*	0.00038	−0.00037	−0.0016
	(1.18)	(−1.07)	(−2.57)	(0.30)	(−0.71)	(−0.34)
POPDEN	0.019	−0.0047	−0.029	0.026	0.0043	0.020
	(0.88)	(−2.05)	(−0.81)	(1.92)	(0.79)	(0.40)
BLACK	−0.057	0.028	−0.18	0.045	0.012	−0.87
	(−0.13)	(0.61)	(−0.25)	(0.12)	(0.085)	(−0.66)
MANUF	−0.13	0.11	0.51	−0.424*	0.060	1.40
	(−0.21)	(1.64)	(0.50)	(−2.13)	(0.74)	(1.92)
PROFMAN	−0.75	0.20	1.64	−1.25*	−0.00036	4.93*
	(−0.74)	(1.84)	(0.99)	(−2.57)	(−0.002)	(2.78)
PUBTRANS	−0.0076	0.089	0.34	−0.15	−0.723	−8.19*
	(−0.008)	(0.85)	(0.21)	(−0.14)	(−1.69)	(−2.13)
MEDAGE	−1.13	0.061	2.86	0.49	0.26	1.57
	(−0.73)	(0.37)	(1.12)	(0.64)	(0.83)	(0.56)
R²	0.350	0.534	0.602	0.526	0.358	0.522
R² adj.	−0.064	0.238	0.348	0.351	0.122	0.346
F Test	0.85	1.80	2.37	3.01*	1.51	2.96*

*Significant at the 0.05 level
**Significant at the 0.01 level
Values in parentheses are *t*-ratios.

Table 7–13. Regressions Relating Seven Independent Variables to Commuting Variables in Non-South Dispersed Urban Regions

Independent Variables	Dependent Variables		
	PERWF	PEROUT	OUTPWF
Constant	−6.91	−8.85	−33.2
AREA	−0.00023	−0.000068	0.000069
	(−0.49)	(−0.93)	(0.062)
POPDEN	−0.0089	0.011	0.078
	(−0.12)	(0.90)	(0.42)
BLACK	−0.142	−0.158	−0.704
	(−0.29)	(−2.01)	(−0.60)
MANUF	0.257	−0.022	−0.33
	(0.603)	(−0.32)	(−0.33)
PROFMAN	−0.013	0.045	0.46
	(−0.026)	(0.55)	(0.38)
PUBTRANS	−1.33	−0.89	−3.18
	(−0.37)	(−1.56)	(−0.37)
MEDAGE	0.670	0.450	1.88
	(0.55)	(2.32)	(0.65)
R^2	0.634	0.850	0.243
R^2 adj.	0.121	0.639	−0.818
F Test	1.24	4.04	0.23

Values in parentheses are *t*-ratios.

Similarly, it was argued at the outset of this chapter that persons in managerial, professional and related activities will commute greater distances because of their larger normal preference areas and the likelihood that their expected level of residential amenities will be met farther from their place of business activity. If this is the case then PROFMAN should be directly related to commuting. Availability and use of public transportation, as reflected in PUBTRANS, should also be directly related to commuting. REGION is a dummy variable to control for South–non-South differences; these areas are assigned values of 1 and 0 respectively. To the extent that poorer economic circumstances in the South inhibit commuting, REGION would be inversely related to commuting. However, simple comparison of the mean commuting values shown in Table 7–6 indicates a tendency for commuters as a proportion of the labor force to be higher in the South, but for commuting outside of region to be lower. Finally, because it has frequently been observed that younger people are more mobile than older people, it was expected that MEDAGE would be inversely related to commuting.

Table 7–10 shows regression results for equations relating the eight independent variables to each of the three commuting variables. Separate results are shown for nonmetropolitan regions, SMSAs and dispersed urban areas.

In terms of the F test, each of the equations for nonmetropolitan regions is significant at the 0.01 level. However, after adjusting the R^2 values for degrees of freedom it is apparent that there is a great deal of unexplained variance in the commuting variables. In the equation with PERWF as the dependent variable, none of the regression coefficients is significant at the 0.05 level. In the equation with PEROUT as the dependent variable, three regression coefficients—AREA, PROFMAN and REGION—are significant at the 0.05 level. AREA and REGION have the hypothesized negative values, but PROFMAN does not, which may reflect the kind of nonmetropolitan areas being considered here. It was pointed out earlier in this chapter that residents of the open country and rural towns depend more on commuting than their counterparts in small cities. For example, only 11 percent of the residents in nonsuburban cities in the 10,000 to 49,999 population range commuted to another county to work; this was less than half the corresponding 24 percent rate for residents of the open country and rural towns. All of our nonmetropolitan regions have at least one city with over 10,000 population and most have a number of cities in the 10,000 to 49,999 range. The fact that PROFMAN is inversely related to PEROUT indicates that these regions are self-contained in terms of the relevant activities.

The nonmetropolitan equation with OUTPWF as the dependent variable has five regression coefficients that are significant—the three just discussed (with the same signs), as well as BLACK and MEDAGE. However, the signs of the last two are not those expected. The explanation in the case of BLACK may be the way in which the dependent variable is defined. The proportion of workers commuting—PERWF—is in fact inversely related to BLACK, as hypothesized. The positive relationship between BLACK and OUTPWF may reflect lack of economic opportunity in areas with a high proportion of blacks; while blacks may have difficulty commuting, those who do often have to go to work places outside of region. The positive sign of MEDAGE may reflect external commuting as a means of adjustment for older workers, but then our nonmetropolitan areas would not be as self-contained for older workers as they appear to be for persons in the professional and managerial categories. This might also apply to the only significant regression coefficient in the equations for dispersed urban areas.

Equations for South and non-South areas are shown in Tables 7–11, 7–12 and 7–13, which refer respectively to nonmetropolitan regions, SMSAs and dispersed urban regions. No equations are shown for the South in Table 7–13 due to lack of a sufficient number of observations. The independent variables are the same as those shown in Table 7–10 except that the regional dummy variable is dropped.

In both Tables 7–11 and 7–12, none of the equations for the South is significant in terms of the F test. Indeed, the only significant regression coefficient is AREA in the equation with OUTPWF as the dependent variable.

For nonmetropolitan regions outside the South (Table 7–11), PROFMAN is significant in all three of the commuting equations; the equations for PEROUT and OUTPWF are each significant at the 0.01 level. The negative signs on the PROFMAN variable have already been discussed.

For non-South SMSAs (Table 7–12), the equations with PERWF and OUTPWF as dependent variables are each significant at the 0.05 level. In the former MANUF and PROFMAN are each significant and inversely related to PERWF. Curiously, PROFMAN is significantly but directly related to OUTPWF. PUBTRANS also is significantly related to OUTPWF. The inverse relationship implies that public transportation is geared to intra-SMSA commuting; the more the use of public transportation the less the proportion of all commuters leaving the SMSA to work. Judging from the negative signs for PUBTRANS in the dispersed urban region equations (Tables 7–10 and 7–13), a similar phenomenon may be at work in them, though the *t*-values are not large enough to be significant.

SUMMARY AND CONCLUSIONS

A major reason for the relatively low income levels and high poverty levels in rural areas and small towns is lack of access to employment opportunities. It is frequently argued that commuting can overcome the access problem and examples can be cited to show that this in fact has happened. However, such examples usually are drawn from two rather special kinds of nonmetropolitan situations—those areas in proximity to SMSAs and those with a fairly large number of persons within commuting distance of one another. The nonmetropolitan regions studied in this chapter belong to the latter category.

Levels of economic well-being in the nonmetropolitan regions—whether measured in terms of median family income or incidence of poverty—were significantly lower than in SMSAs or dispersed urban regions. The SMSAs selected for comparison were usually those closest to the respective nonmetropolitan regions, though they were not within normal commuting distance. For the most part they were of medium size; only four had a population over one million. The dispersed urban regions were relatively large in area and consisted of clusters or axes of small and medium-size cities together with intervening nonmetropolitan counties.

Despite economic conditions that make private automobile ownership difficult and despite the paucity of public transportation in rural areas, a surprising number of rural workers nevertheless commute to work. Indeed, the number of commuters as a proportion of the total reporting work force is not significantly different among nonmetropolitan regions, SMSAs and dispersed urban regions. Moreover, the proportion of commuters is greater in the nonmetropolitan South than in other nonmetropolitan regions, even though median family income is significantly lower and poverty incidence significantly higher. Measures of commuting out of region also indicate that long distance commuting is significantly greater in nonmetropolitan regions than in SMSAs or dispersed urban regions.

The regression analyses suggest that the kinds of nonmetropolitan regions being considered here are relatively self-contained for professional and managerial categories of residents, but not for black and older workers. Blacks appear to have difficulty commuting and those few who do often have to go to work places outside of their region. The proportion of commuters who leave nonmetropolitan regions is significantly and directly related to median age.

Lack of public transportation obviously is particularly detrimental to disadvantaged rural workers; and the energy crisis certainly will make access to jobs via private automobile even more difficult. Within the kinds of nonmetropolitan regions being considered—they have at least 100,000 persons within commuting range of one another—it should be possible to organize transportation systems to link more effectively the unemployed and underemployed with employment opportunities, especially in view of the mobility exhibited by rural workers who have the means to commute. But transportation, no matter how necessary, is only one element in what must be a constellation of change involving the coordination of complementary activities among numerous units of government and greater attention to the manpower and human resource needs of nonmetropolitan residents.

NOTES

[1] Anthony J. Catanese, "Commuting Behavior Patterns of Families," *Traffic Quarterly* 24, 3 (July 1970): 446–48.

[2] Kenneth McLennan and Paul Seidenstat, *New Businesses and Urban Employment Opportunities* (Lexington, Mass.: D.C. Heath Lexington Books, 1972), p. 159.

[3] Catanese, p. 455.

[4] Richard E. Lonsdale, "Two North Carolina Commuting Patterns," *Economic Geography* 42, 2 (April 1966): 115.

[5] Calvin L. Beale, "Rural Development: Population and Settlement Prospects," *Journal of Soil and Water Conservation* 29, 1 (January-February 1974): 25–26.

[6] Ibid., p. 26.

[7] John Fraser Hart, Neil E. Salisbury and Everett G. Smith, Jr., "The Dying Village and Some Notions About Urban Growth," *Economic Geography* 44, 4 (October 1968): 343–49.

[8] Ira Kaye, "Introduction," *The Transportation of People in Rural Areas*, Committee Print prepared for the Subcommittee on Rural Development, Committee on Agriculture and Forestry, U.S. Senate, 93rd Cong., 2nd sess., February 27, 1974 (Washington, D.C.: Government Printing Office, 1974), p. 2.

[9] John H. Holmes, "Linkages Between External Commuting and Out-Migration: Evidence from Middle-Eastern Pennsylvania," *Economic Geography* 48, 4 (October 1972): 406–20.

[10] John H. Holmes, "External Commuting as a Prelude to Suburbanization," *Annals of the Association of American Geographers* 61, 4 (December 1971): 790.

[11] Ibid.

[12] Wilbur R. Thompson, "The Economic Base of Urban Problems," in Neil W. Chamberlain, ed., *Contemporary Economic Issues* (Homewood, Ill.: Richard D. Irwin, Inc., 1969), pp. 25–26.

[13] Ibid., p. 26.

[14] Kaye, p. 1.

[15] Sanford H. Bederman and John S. Adams, "Job Accessibility and Underemployment," *Annals of the Association of American Geographers* 64, 3 (September 1974): 378–86.

[16] Ibid., p. 378.

[17] The commuting data presented in the remainder of this chapter were computed from data furnished by the Bureau of Economic Analysis, U. S. Department of Commerce.

Chapter Eight

Innovations in Rural Transportation

Throughout this study, but especially in the chapter just concluded, considerable attention has been given to the role of transportation in providing nonmetropolitan workers increased access to manpower services and employment opportunities. However, it also has been emphasized that transportation is only one part of a more general pattern of development that must take place if the relative disadvantages of nonmetropolitan areas are to be reduced—if not entirely overcome—in the foreseeable future. The conclusions presented in the next chapter are developed in this more general context. First, though, more detailed consideration will be given in this chapter to innovative means for linking manpower and transportation programs in nonmetropolitan areas.

RURAL TRANSPORTATION AND RURAL POVERTY

For most Americans transportation is not a luxury but a necessity; nevertheless, it is either not available to many rural families at a price they can afford or else not convenient. In most instances the provision of transportation is not in itself sufficient to eliminate poverty, yet lack of transportation can contribute significantly to isolation and ignorance of public services and employment opportunities. Thus, transportation programs need to be an integral part of any serious attempt to improve economic and social conditions in rural areas.

The results presented in the preceding chapter clearly indicated that rural people are as willing to commute to work as their urban counterparts, and perhaps even more so. That rural people are as wedded to the automobile as Americans in general is illustrated by the fact that there are proportionally as many households with two or three automobiles in rural areas as there are in urban areas, although per capita income is lower and poverty incidence is higher in rural areas. Even in the disadvantaged groups of elderly persons, handicapped persons and poor adults the proportions of households without automobiles is lower in rural areas. However, these comparisons are misleading because the number of reliable automobiles is less in rural areas; average automobile age is greater in rural areas and many poor rural households keep essentially unusable vehicles on their property.[1] In addition, the rural resident has relatively less chance to use trains, subways, taxis and buses. Intercity buses serving major urban markets do not effectively serve rural areas; their schedules are not geared to rural-to-urban commuting or to the daily trip purposes of rural residents. Rural bus systems are few and far between; in the early 1970s the majority of such systems were operated as experimental or demonstration projects, but they have been drastically curtailed because of cutbacks from their principal source of funding—the Office of Economic Opportunity. Although taxis in most small towns stretch their coverage to surrounding areas, population densities are generally too low to permit economical use of conventional taxi services. Thus, it has been estimated that rural poor people make only 15 percent of the total trips made by the average American.[2]

The mode of transportation used most frequently by rural poor people to reach areas of job opportunities is the carpool. In 1970, two out of every five poor rural workers used this form of travel to work.[3] Carpools

are organized through informal association with friends and neighbors, and when the vehicles are reliable, have worked quite well. Reliability is the problem. Often the vehicle is old, maintenance is poor or non-existent, repairs and good tires are too expensive. With the reliability of this pool of shared-ride vehicles so low, the entry-level worker is likely to be replaced by another employee if he is late or fails to show for work too often.[4]

The data in Table 8–1 show the proportions of family income spent for various budget categories in 1970, by urban-rural residence and by poverty-nonpoverty status within rural areas. For rural poor residents the proportion spent for transportation averaged 10.8 percent. This was less than the corresponding proportions for urban residents and for rural nonpoor families. The relatively high proportion (17.4 percent) spent by rural nonpoor residents on transportation reflects the fact that in general rural residents drive longer distances to work; in 1970, 23 percent of rural workers were employed outside of their county of residence, whereas this was the case for only 18 percent of workers living in urban areas. The relatively low proportion spent by rural poor people on transportation may reflect in part greater reliance on carpooling than among other groups. However, the more likely explanation is that rural poor people simply are not frequently found among the long distance commuting population.

Table 8-1. Average Annual Family Expenditures for Specific Current Consumption, by Urban-Rural Family Residence and by Rural Poverty Status, 1970

	Percentage of Annual Budget			
			Rural	
Item	*All families*	*All urban*	*Poor*	*Nonpoor*
Food, beverages, tobaco	23.2	22.9	29.4	21.7
Clothing and personal	11.7	12.1	9.6	11.2
Housing	28.7	29.4	28.8	25.9
Medical care	7.6	7.4	10.5	7.0
Transportation	12.6	11.6	10.8	17.4
Recreation	6.5	7.8	1.8	3.6
Other	9.6	8.8	9.1	13.2

Source: Edwin W. Hauser et al., *The Use of Existing Facilities for Transporting Disadvantaged Residents of Rural Areas,* vol. 2 (Raleigh, N.C.: Kimley-Horn and Associates for the Federal Highway Administration, October 31, 1974), p. 2–14.

Typically they remain unemployed or underemployed in the local labor market and they spend relatively high proportions of their budgets on food and medical care.

OFFICE OF ECONOMIC OPPORTUNITY RURAL TRANSPORTATION DEMONSTRATION PROJECTS

In the late 1960s the Office of Economic Opportunity, in pursuit of its objective of helping to lift people out of poverty, provided demonstration grants to a number of rural transportation prototype systems. By 1972 about 50 such projects were being operated under the auspices of local community action agencies, which had consistently identified transportation as a major problem area. Because of cutbacks in OEO funding most of these projects have either disappeared or else have been severely curtailed. However, even with subsidies it was evident that there were few people, even among the target populations, who were willing *and able* to pay for transportation services.

In general, rural transit systems cannot be expected to be self-supporting. Revenue rarely comes close to the 12 cents per passenger mile which typifies the costs of the system. Costs are high because low population density and a multiplicity of destinations in most rural areas result in high per passenger cost for driver salaries and management. Ridership on subsidized systems, which have been set up under OEO and similar auspices, tends to be a small fraction either of the general population or even of the "disadvantaged" population. Competition from auto alternatives (carpooling, ridesharing, etc.) diminishes the effective demand for transit solutions. It is difficult to get programmatic consensus on destinations because of conflicting alternatives, and ridership is low as a consequence.

A subsidy large enough to provide "minimum service levels" to all the disadvantaged in a region is beyond what appears to be the fiscal capacity of local governments in rural areas. Few of the original OEO experiments have been picked up for sustained local funding.

It may be useful in light of these findings to restrict new expenditures of "rural demonstration" monies to low-cost innovations such as (1) systematized carpooling, (2) transportation vouchers for specific target populations, or (3) consolidating social service transportation and service delivery programs.[5]

At this writing, it appears that funds authorized under Section 147 of the Federal Highway Act of 1973 for demonstration rural public highway transportation programs will be appropriated. About $10 million will be allocated to strictly demonstration programs in various regions to help learn more about how to provide better public transportation in rural areas. Their design should benefit from the lessons of the OEO experience. For example, the low effective demand (as contrasted with considerable need) for rural transportation services has several critical implications. "First, whatever transit service is provided must be no more than required to meet whatever objective it is designed to achieve. Second, it must be very carefully tailored to serve specific types of trips. Third, its costs must be kept as low as possible. Therefore, the planner of rural transit must begin with a fairly firm idea of what he intends to accomplish."[6]

In most of the OEO-funded projects, a major trip type involved poor and elderly persons seeking access to shopping, medical and social service facilities. Such trips were usually made infrequently but with considerable advance knowledge. The destinations were usually few and concentrated, and often a single town; origins were more numerous and dispersed because potential riders tended to be more scattered and more isolated than the general population. A second type of transportation service involved regular trips made to social service program facilities, especially Head Start and adult training programs. Their regularity allowed for prescheduling through the agencies involved. General transit trips comprise a third category of transportation services. These occurred when a combination of random individual trips resulted in a demand great enough to support a transit service. The appropriate conditions were usually found only between fairly large concentrations of population. Finally, work trips were provided in only a few projects, largely because most employed persons had their own cars or had made carpooling arrangements. In the cases where work trips were involved, there was a single large employer or a concentration of employers employing a substantial number of low income workers, many of whom were women. Moreover, workers' residences were usually sufficiently concentrated to allow for very simple pickup. Very often the rural transportation services were designed to include more than one trip type. Although this approach required some compromise, it was important, if difficult, to identify the origins, destinations, frequencies and times that potential riders would wish to make each type of trip. Costly household surveys usually produced exaggerated estimates of potential demand. The simplest means for identifying concentrations of potential users was to use census data and available local information, especially data from social service agencies. One relatively successful technique was to advertize that a transportation service was being planned and ask those interested to telephone stating the specific services they would use. This approach reduced significantly the misleading responses typically obtained in household surveys.[7]

Once determination is made of what a rural transportation system is to accomplish, it is essential that a rational pricing system be established. Under private ownership it is important that the system show a profit, or at least break even. In contrast, government agencies tend to view the problem as one of moving people between their residences and the places where they want or need to go. In consequence, they often have subsidized transportation systems deemed vital to the public interest. But the very knowledge that the system is subsidized has led to relaxed efficiency standards and uneconomic practices.

It is generally accepted that vehicles must have loads of one-half to two-thirds of capacity if they are to break even, and that the fewer the seats in the vehicle, the higher must be the per seat price to cover driver, management and maintenance costs. As in the case of lunches, there are no free rides. Some agency must absorb the cost if a ride is provided at no charge. In general, pricing should be based on the costs of operation; any other practice tends to lead to eventual bankruptcy and no service for anyone. If economic realities are to be respected, agencies wishing to discount services to a specific group should be issued full price tickets; the cost would thus be defrayed by the agency and not by the transportation system. One exception might be to reduce prices for certain groups—e.g., older persons—during low usage periods. Although a small cost might be involved, it would not be enough to threaten the financial soundness of the system, and this practice could contribute to a good public image.[8]

CETA AND RURAL TRANSPORTATION: A MODEL PROGRAM IN SOUTH CAROLINA

Considerable attention has been given to improving access to social services in rural areas, and this certainly is vital to upgrading rural human resources. Unfortunately, relatively little attention has been given to access to manpower services in rural areas.

> Labor is finding it more and more difficult to economically reach places of employment which have increasingly become more distant from home. Manpower training programs have not been able to affect the unemployed who, for this economic reason, are unable to reach the classes. Rural youth wishing to acquire advanced educations, especially at vocational-technical schools, are some of the more seriously affected since the lack of any other means forces them to spend what they might have saved for educational purposes on an old car, gas, and oil, a temptation that is always present in any case.[9]

In a similar vein, a recent study of rural transportation concludes that "virtually all of the rural transportation operations are in fact social service delivery systems. If rural public transportation systems are to provide employment facilitation, then different systems than those currently existing must be planned."[10]

Perhaps the most innovative program to adapt rural transportation to manpower service delivery is that currently being implemented in South Carolina with CETA funds. A study analyzing the transportation needs of rural poor people in five states—Arizona, Minnesota, Missouri, North Carolina and South Carolina—found that "persons in Minnesota consider themselves relatively well off and do not perceive transportation as much of a problem. In South Carolina, on the other hand, people seem to be convinced that lack of transportation plays a big role in their lives and that things would be much better if they did have adequate transportation."[11] Although this conclusion was not drawn in the specific context of manpower services, it does indicate that the new South Carolina program is directed toward a population with a high perceived need for transportation.

In 1974, South Carolina established a rural transportation system to serve manpower program enrollees, although other rural people in need of transportation can also use it when space is available. The system is a cooperative effort between the state's office of manpower planning and coordination (OMPC), which is lodged in the office of the governor, and 11 transportation contractors in ten substate planning districts.[12]

Prior to the implementation of the Comprehensive Employment and Training Act of 1973 (CETA), the South Carolina Office of the Governor was named state prime sponsor for a special one year pilot grant from the U.S. Department of Labor. This pilot project—termed the Comprehensive Manpower Program (CMP)—received over $12 million in federal funds; it was intended to show how a coordinated and comprehensive approach could be taken in delivering a wide range of manpower services, including intake, classroom training, subsidized public employment, subsidized private employment, and work experience and services. At the outset, the approach taken to the transportation of manpower program enrollees was to reimburse them on a per mile traveled basis and let them find their own transportation between their residences and the sites where relevant services were delivered. However, it soon became clear that a great deal of the absenteeism in classroom training, work experience and other program components was related to transportation, medical and child care needs. Moreover, enrollees were not coming from rural areas, but from metropolitan areas; and the use of most existing public transportation vehicles was highly restricted so that manpower enrollees usually could not use them. In response, OMPC purchased 40 new vehicles with CMP funds and assigned them to subcontractors for operation. However, before all of the vehicles had been delivered the CMP grant expired and was replaced by CETA as a primary funding source. Under CETA, the counties of Greenville, Spartanburg, Anderson, Charleston, Lexington and Richland, as well as the city of Columbia, joined with the office of the governor to form a statewide prime sponsorship. Again OMPC became the prime sponsor and was in a position to implement its plan for statewide transportation for manpower clients.

At this time OMPC hired the services of a consultant to help plan the statewide transportation system. The consultant helped to set up the cost accounting and bookkeeping systems of the transportation contracts, to design vehicle maintenance schedules, to allocate vehicles according to need, to design a contract instrument and to train the OMPC staff on the operation of a transportation system. Meanwhile, the U.S. Department of Labor gave its permission to operate general purpose vehicles with first priority to manpower enrollees, but with the understanding that passengers not in manpower programs could be carried where space was available.

The basis for the selection of agencies to be transportation contractors was their ability to operate a transportation system in the substate planning districts and their desire to cooperate with OMPC in setting up a system. Eleven contractors were chosen; most are community action agencies (CAAs), but they also include other community-based organizations and one county unit of government. The present contractors and the counties that they serve are as follows:

Agency	*Counties Served*
Greenville CAA	Oconee, Pickens, Anderson, Greenville
Piedmont CAA	Spartanburg, Cherokee
GLEAMS CAA	Abbeville, Laurens, Greenwood, McCormick, Saluda, Edgefield

Carolina CAA	York, Chester, Union, Lancaster
Richland County (Columbia)	Newberry, Richland, Fairfield, Lexington
Aiken-Edgefield CAA	Aiken, Barnwell
Orangeburg CAA	Calhoun, Orangeburg, Bamberg, Allendale
Wateree CAA	Kershaw, Lee, Sumter, Clarendon
Darlington CAA	Chesterfield, Darlington, Marlboro, Dillon, Florence, Marion
Horry-Georgetown Economic Opportunity Commission	Horry, Georgetown, Williamsburg
None	Charleston, Berkeley, Dorchester
Beaufort-Jasper Comprehensive Health Agency	Beaufort, Jasper, Hampton, Colleton

The original fleet of forty 15 passenger maxivans was put into operation in August 1974. In addition, 22 old vehicles were allocated to the contractors. These old vehicles, which ranged in size from 54 passenger buses to station wagons, frequently had more than 100,000 miles on them and were inherited from the old concentrated employment program around the state. All of them were in relatively poor condition and thus they could only be used as back-up vehicles. Early in 1975, four emergency vehicles were provided the Columbia area, and eleven 28 passenger vehicles and 13 new 15 passenger vans were distributed throughout the system. No more purchases were planned for the immediate future. The estimated replacement cost of the entire fleet of 68 new vehicles and 22 back-up units is $401,000. All vehicles carry federal license tags and drivers also must possess federal licenses. Title to all of the vehicles is retained by the U.S. Department of Labor.

During fiscal year 1975, dollar ceilings on transportation contracts ranged from $12,250 for the Aiken-Edgefield CAA, which operates in only two counties, to $35,346 for the Greenville CAA, which serves four counties. An unusual feature of the South Carolina program is that payment for manpower enrollee transportation is on a passenger mile basis rather than on the vehicle mile basis favored by other state agencies providing client transportation. Contractors are reimbursed at 6 cents per passenger mile for OMPC enrollees only; the schedule is calculated at a rate of 60 cents per vehicle mile and assumes a two-thirds average capacity load on a 15 passenger van. Out of this reimbursement the contractor is expected to cover the costs of fuel, maintenance, drivers' salaries and repairs. Driver costs are minimal in most cases because manpower enrollees drive the vehicles. This procedure has come under the fire of state auditors who want contractors reimbursed at actual cost. The rationale for the present system is that it provides an incentive to contractors to do their best in providing efficient, effective routing and scheduling, thereby eliminating "deadheading" as much as possible. As might be expected, practice has shown that it is easier to eliminate deadheading when enrollees are located in proximity to each other, and this happens most frequently in relatively urban areas. In view of these considerations it is likely that the 6 cents per passenger mile reimbursement will be altered in favor of a schedule that allows for rural-urban differences in intensity of vehicle utilization and for the auditors' insistence that the contractors' accounts should show neither surplus nor loss on balance over time. The reimbursement rate would thus be raised in rural areas such as Beaufort, where there is a considerable amount of deadheading and where vehicles travel relatively long distances with fewer than ten passengers, the assumed number if the maxivans were to maintain ridership at two-thirds of vehicle capacity.

It makes no difference if manpower enrollees ride on OMPC vehicles or on other vehicles operated by the transportation contractors so long as the vehicles are in good operating condition. This feature gives the contractor a high degree of flexibility in routing and scheduling his vehicles. A related feature of the contract is that OMPC vehicles may be used to transport clients other than manpower enrollees, provided that the latter have all been served first. The contractor can thus obtain additional revenues by contracting excess capacity to other state agencies, or other organizations, to transport their clients at whatever rate can be arranged.

Another unusual aspect of the contracting instrument is a set of three deductions for, respectively, equipment depreciation, insurance and management counseling. The rationale is to build up a replacement fund for worn out vehicles and to reimburse OMPC for the insurance policy and management consulting that it front-ended. These deductions are tied to vehicle miles instead of passenger miles because regardless of whether OMPC clients or non-OMPC clients are being transported, the relevant costs are related to the operation of the vehicle.

Contractors contribute 4.5 cents of federal Department of Labor funds per vehicle mile to the equipment depreciation fund; this amount is deducted from the 6 cents per passenger mile reimbursement paid to contractors for OMPC enrollees. The equipment depreciation fund is intended to be used to replace vehicles that have over 100,000 miles of use. However, this procedure may have to be eliminated because of the doubtful legality of using federal money for this type of contingency fund. Contractors also contribute eight-tenths of a cent of Department of Labor funds per vehicle mile to the insurance fund, though the total contribution to this fund is not to exceed $200 per vehicle. The purpose of this procedure is to pay back OMPC's front-ended costs of $21,610 for insurance on its fleet of vehicles. Finally, contractors contribute one-half cent per vehicle mile up to $500 per vehicle to defray OMPC's costs for providing technical, managerial and general transportation system development assistance to the respective contractors.

The scope of services to be provided by the contractors primarily involves transporting manpower program enrollees from their homes to Tec (State Board for Technical and Comprehensive Education) centers and back. However, it sometimes involves transporting whole classes—e.g., enrollees in home repair courses are transported as a group between work sites and Tec centers. Occasionally it also involves transporting enrollees in other manpower programs—e.g., work experience programs. Contractors may carry manpower enrollees in non-OMPC vehicles if they meet safety standards, and, as has already been pointed out, they may carry passengers other than manpower enrollees in OMPC vans on a space available basis.

At this writing, total investment in terms of federal funds obligated for the transportation system has been $711,751, which includes insurance, vehicles, management consultant and operating cost contracts. An additional $136,122 of CETA funds has been spent for travel allowances. These represent a 10 cent per vehicle mile reimbursement to manpower enrollees for transportation from their homes to pickup points in areas where the OMPC transportation exists, and from homes to manpower program facilities in the Charleston area, where OMPC does not have a transportation system. With the exception of the Charleston area, travel allowances will soon be discontinued. If they were not continued in Charleston there would be a danger that it would break away from the state prime sponsorship arrangement to become a prime sponsor in its own right.

AN EVALUATION OF THE SOUTH CAROLINA OMPC PROGRAM

The OMPC rural public transportation program is still too new and too modest in scope to permit definitive evaluation. At the end of January 1975 the various transportation contractors reported that they were carrying 462 manpower enrollees daily, as well as 108 non-OMPC passengers per day on OMPC vehicles. My interviews with OMPC officials in the capital and with several of the contractors indicated general satisfaction with the program. In most areas the access of rural persons to manpower services would be greatly diminished or even nonexistent without the program.

In some areas the 6 cent per passenger mile reimbursement given to contractors is considered inadequate because it is not feasible to maintain an average of ten manpower enrollee riders per trip. Even if ten or more enrollees are delivered to a Tec center by one van, many of the riders are picked up only toward the end of the trip—i.e., the first part of the trip is not economical for contractors reimbursed on a passenger mile basis. Some contractors also object to the magnitude of the paper work involved in keeping track of passenger miles of service; they would prefer to have a contract with a flat reimbursement total. However, these objections are relatively minor in relation to the main advantage of the program from the contractors' viewpoint—the use of OMPC vans as general purpose vehicles.

OMPC has recommended to the South Carolina legislature that it go on record to request all state agencies involved in rural transportation to lift special requirements on their vehicles so that they may be used for multiple purposes. This may entail a special request by the legislature or the governor to the federal agencies involved to follow the example of the U.S. Department of Labor in allowing vehicles to be used for general purposes.

It should be emphasized that all parties involved in the operation of the OMPC program favor the depreciation fund as a means for assuring that vehicles can be replaced when they wear out. If the fund is not permitted by state or federal auditors, there is a real danger that this imaginative program to help disadvantaged people in rural areas will not be able to fulfill its promise and that it will become yet another ephemeral, one-shot project.

Even if the South Carolina OMPC program does prove to be a successful model for an expanded national program, rural transportation is only one element in the total problem of creating greater access to economic opportunity in rural areas. But at least within the realm of rural public transportation, the OMPC program is noteworthy because while it addresses the needs of manpower program enrollees, it also is sufficiently flexible to serve more comprehensive needs. There remains the task of creating a more comprehensive and systematic framework for dealing effectively with these needs. As an eminent rural transportation authority points out:

Until we achieve a national growth policy . . . it is doubtful whether Congress will (or should) authorize funds necessary to provide public transportation for rural people. Mini-programs which just reach narrowly defined groups of people like the elderly, poor, mentally retarded, etc., will proliferate for awhile and then phase out, leaving a void. All such special groups will be better served by a truly comprehensive system, flexible enough to take care of the special needs.[13]

A NOTE ON THE ENERGY CRISIS AND RURAL AREAS

As in the rest of the nation, people in rural areas have become highly dependent on energy from fossil fuels for both production and household consumption. It is likely that household consuming units in rural areas will be more adversely affected by higher fuel prices than those in urban areas. The proportion of a family's income spent directly or indirectly for energy is inversely related to level of income. Food, housing and transportation account for about three-quarters of the energy consumption of a typical household. However, because low income families spend proportionally more on these items than other families, their dependence on energy is relatively greater. Thus, an increase in the cost of energy has a relatively great effect on low income families. And because rural incomes are lower than urban incomes, the impact of higher energy costs will be proportionally greater among the rural population. According to one estimate,

about 14 percent of all consumption expenditures of rural households is accounted for by direct and indirect energy costs. This is about one-eighth again the share of metropolitan area income devoted to energy consumption. Assuming a perfectly inelastic demand, this means a 50 percent increase in energy costs would result in an increase in household expenses of about seven percent.[14]

Similarly, Bradley Perry has estimated changes in welfare associated with higher fuel prices by measuring the increase in per capita income required to maintain existing levels of personal consumption outlays. The findings indicate that the per capita welfare of rural residents declines about one-fourth more than that of urban residents, largely because of the greater dependence of rural people on the automobile for transportation and on fuel oil for home heating.[15]

The effects of the energy crisis on nonmetropolitan employment are uncertain, but rough estimates have been made with the INFORUM input-output model. Assuming a doubling of the 1973 price of crude petroleum and using an 87 industry matrix (see Table 8–2), the model predicts a net loss of about 8000 jobs in nonmetropolitan areas. However, there would be a larger reallocation among rural industries. There is a predicted loss of 142,000 rural jobs in some industries and a gain of 134,000 rural jobs in other industries. The data in Table 8–2 indicate that of the 29 sectors that have 30 percent or more of their employment located in rural areas, only a

Table 8–2. Impact of Increased Energy Costs on Rural Employment and Selected Energy Data

Definition of ranks a through g: a—rank applies to the miscellaneous textile and floor covering industry as a whole; b—rank applies to the millwork and plywood and miscellaneous wood products industry as a whole; c—rank applies to the food and kindred products industry as a whole; d—3 industries are tied for rank; e—rank applies to the chemical industry as a whole; f—rank applies to the rubber industry as a whole; g—rank applies to the professional, scientific and controlling instrument industry as a whole.

		Industry ranks in use of refined petroleum products, energy and fuel purchased, by industry			
Industry listing by degree of rurality[1]	*Potential net change in rural area jobs due to doubling of petroleum prices, 1973–74 (thousands of jobs)*[2]	*Direct use of refined petroleum products (1970)*[3]	*Direct requirements of refined petroleum products per worker (1970)*[3]	*Dollar amount of energy and fuel purchased (1971)*[4]	*Energy and fuel costs as a percent of value of shipments (1971)*[4]
1. Logging and lumber (78)	−3	24	23	11	8
2. Agriculture (72)	9	5	14	—	—
3. Floor coverings (61)	2	a50	a31	60	28
4. Mining (61)	9	19	16	—	—
5. Petroleum and gas (56)	−19	21	15	—	—
6. Fabrics and yarn (53)	9	36	53	9	9
7. Trailers, cycles (53)	2	63	64	68	72
8. Plywood, millwork, etc (48)	−2	b52	b60	21	17
9. Wooden containers (48)	0	b52	b60	74	21
10. Sugar (48)	0	c11	c22	40	11
11. Footwear and other leather (43)	−1	d61	d69	65	68
12. Knit fabric and apparel (39)	7	57	62	36	30
13. Paper and prod. fx. containers (38)	−2	16	17	4	4
14. Farm machinery (38)	2	55	44	52	41
15. Canned and frozen foods (37)	0	c11	c22	16	29
16. Plastics and synthetics (36)	−1	12	4	8	5
17. Furniture (35)	−2	53	68	25	39
18. Miscellaneous textiles (34)	−1	a50	a31	53	16
19. Construction (new and old) (34)	0	2	12	—	—
20. Meat (34)	0	c11	c20	14	71
21. Apparel (33)	21	54	71	24	70
22. Household appliances (33)	−1	56	51	46	53
23. Grain mill products (32)	0	c11	c22	19	27
24. Agricultural chemicals (32)	0	31	9	42	12
25. Railroads (31)	5	10	6	—	—
26. Stone and clay products (31)	−3	17	18	3	3
27. Electric utilities (30)	−2	8	5	—	—
28. Natural gas, water and sewer (30)	0	20	11	—	—
29. Leather and ind. leather products (30)	0	d61	d69	70	13
30. Dairy (28)	0	c11	c20	18	43
31. Trucking (27)	−2	7	10	—	—
32. Wholesale and retail trade (27)	64	1	30	—	—
33. Radio, TV sets and phono (27)	−2	64	54	67	73
34. Glue, ink and fatty acid (26)	0	e3	e1	26	10
35. Glass and glass products (24)	−1	d61	d69	73	50
36. Tobacco (24)	0	67	61	64	74
37. Finance and services (23)	−46	4	38	—	—
38. Nonferrous metals (23)	−2	15	13	6	6

Table 8–2. continued

Definition of ranks a through g: a—rank applies to the miscellaneous textile and floor covering industry as a whole; b—rank applies to the millwork and plywood and miscellaneous wood products industry as a whole; c—rank applies to the food and kindred products industry as a whole; d—3 industries are tied for rank; e—rank applies to the chemical industry as a whole; f—rank applies to the rubber industry as a whole; g—rank applies to the professional, scientific and controlling instrument industry as a whole.

Industry listing by degree of rurality[1]	Potential net change in rural area jobs due to doubling of petroleum prices, 1973–74 (thousands of jobs)[2]	Industry ranks in use of refined petroleum products, energy and fuel purchased, by industry			
		Direct use of refined petroleum products (1970)[3]	Direct requirements of refined petroleum products per worker (1970)[3]	Dollar amount of energy and fuel purchased (1971)[4]	Energy and fuel costs as a percent of value of shipments (1971)[4]
39. Plastic products (23)	−11	47	50	13	14
40. Rubber products ex. tires (22)	−1	f46	f48	38	15
41. Construction, mine, material handling equipment (22)	−1	40	42	33	52
42. Railroad equipment (22)	1	59	29	69	55
43. Communication (22)	−1	14	26	—	—
44. Plumbing and heating (22)	−1	65	47	62	32
45. Electric appliances and motors (21)	−1	41	33	37	20
46. Engines and turbines (21)	0	45	24	54	56
47. Electronic components (21)	0	49	55	28	26
48. Industrial chemicals (21)	0	e3	e1	2	1
49. General industrial machinery (20)	−1	28	28	29	33
50. Service industry machinery (20)	−1	48	34	44	57
51. Batteries, X-ray equipment, etc (20)	0	39	52	57	45
52. Tires and tubes (19)	0	f46	f48	34	18
53. Household textiles and upholstery (19)	−3	69	70	59	61
54. Newspapers (19)	−1	37	56	48	64
55. Miscellaneous food products (19)	0	e11	c20	12	25
56. Electric lighting and wiring (18)	−1	29	21	50	37
57. Other transport (18)	2	9	7	—	—
58. Special industrial machinery (17)		33	25	47	40
59. Beverages (16)		e11	c20	20	44
60. Transformers, switchgear, el. msr. (16)	−1	44	36	55	54
61. Surgical and medical instruments (16)	0	70	67	71	62
62. Miscellaneous manufacturing (16)	0	34	46	27	49
63. Miscellaneous machinery and shops (15)	−2	60	65	45	22
64. Petroleum refining (15)	−1	(5)	(5)	5	7
65. Iron and steel (15)	−3	13	20	1	2
66. Structural metal products (15)	−1	30	43	23	42
67. Paper containers (15)	0	27	19	31	31
68. Motor vehicles (14)	−11	23	35	7	69
69. Hardware, plating, wire products (14)	−2	26	32	10	19
70. Metalworking machinery (14)	−2	35	39	30	23
71. Ships and boats (14)	0	62	59	58	35
72. Stampings (14)	−2	38	45	22	24
73. Office and computing machinery (13)	−1	51	57	51	67
74. Engineering and scientific instruments (12)	0	g58	g58	72	36
75. Mechanical measuring devices (12)	0	g58	g58	66	51
76. Ordnance (12)	0	42	37	41	46

Table 8–2. continued

Definition of ranks a through g: a—rank applies to the miscellaneous textile and floor covering industry as a whole; b—rank applies to the millwork and plywood and miscellaneous wood products industry as a whole; c—rank applies to the food and kindred products industry as a whole; d—3 industries are tied for rank; e—rank applies to the chemical industry as a whole; f—rank applies to the rubber industry as a whole; g—rank applies to the professional, scientific and controlling instrument industry as a whole.

		Industry ranks in use of refined petroleum products, energy and fuel purchased, by industry			
Industry listing by degree of rurality[1]	*Potential net change in rural area jobs due to doubling of petroleum prices, 1973–74 (thousands of jobs)*[2]	*Direct use of refined petroleum products (1970)*[3]	*Direct requirements of refined petroleum products per worker (1970)*[3]	*Dollar amount of energy and fuel purchased (1971)*[4]	*Energy and fuel costs as a percent of value of shipments (1971)*[4]
77. Bakery (10)	0	11	c20	35	34
78. Drugs (10)	0	43	27	39	38
79. Printing and publishing (9)	−3	32	49	15	59
80. Candy (9)	0	c11	c20	61	48
81. Optical and photographic (8)	0	63	63	49	60
82. Aircraft (7)	1	25	40	17	58
83. Communication equipment (7)	0	66	66	32	65
84. Cleaning and toilet items (6)	0	22	8	43	66
85. Metal containers (6)	0	d61	d41	56	47
86. Paints and allied products (4)	0	18	3	63	63
87. Airlines (2)	0	6	2	—	—

*1. The figures in parentheses refer to the proportion of employment located in nonmetropolitan areas in 1967 for the respective manufacturing industries; for other industries the percentage refers to the proportion of employed people in the respective industry residing in nonmetropolitan areas in 1970.

2. See footnote No. 2.

3. Derived from Ronald E. Kutscher and Charles T. Bowman, "Industrial Use of Petroleum: Effect on Employment," *Monthly Labor Review,* March 1974, pp. 3–8.

4. Derived from data on the costs of purchased fuels and electric energy by industry as provided by economic stabilization program, Cost of Living Council, December 26, 1974.

5. Represents primarily shipments between establishments in the fined petroleum products industry.

Source: The Effects of Uncertain Energy Supplies on Rural Economic Development, Subcommittee on Rural Development, U.S. Senate Committee on Agriculture and Forestry, 93d Cong., 2d sess., September 27, 1974 (Washington, D.C.: Government Printing Office, 1974), pp. 71–72.

few are significant gainers or losers of employment. Eleven sectors lose jobs, nine gain and nine show no change. The petroleum and gas sector shows a loss of 19,000 jobs; no other sector among the 29 most rural sectors shows a loss of over 3000 jobs. Among the gainers the apparel industry stands out, with an increase of 21,000 jobs. Agriculture, mining, and the fabric and yarns sectors each have gains of 9000 jobs, while the knit fabrics sector has a gain of 7000 jobs.

While these estimates are highly tentative, they suggest that the disruptive effects of the energy crisis on nonmetropolitan employment may not be particularly great, especially when the predicted changes are related to total nonmetropolitan employment and to labor adjustments brought on by other causes. Of course, the seriousness of the disruptive influences of the energy crisis will also depend on the degree to which the adverse effects are spread widely or else concentrated within a relatively few places.

Finally, while it is still too early to understand the nature and significance of the broad spatial ramifications of the energy crisis, it is quite possible that it will slow, if not reverse, the decentralizing tendencies discussed in Chapter Two. Proposals to improve the efficiency of energy use in transportation nearly always favor high density or clustered activities.

NOTES

[1] Edwin W. Hauser et al., *The Use of Existing Facilities for Transporting Disadvantaged Residents of Rural Areas*, vol. 2 (Raleigh, N.C.: Kimley-Horn and Associates for the Federal Highway Administration, October 31, 1974), p. 2–8.

[2] Jon E. Burkhardt et al., *A Study of the Transportation Problems of the Rural Poor*, vol. 1 (Bethesda, Md.: Resource Management Corporation for the Office of Economic Opportunity, January 7, 1972), p. 1.

[3] Hauser et al., p. 3–35.

[4] Ibid., p. 2–6.

[5] Alice E. Kidder, "The Economics of Rural Public Transportation Programs" (Paper Presented to the 54th Annual Meeting, Transportation Research Board, Washington, D.C., January 1975), p. 10.

[6] *The Transportation of People in Rural Areas*, Subcommittee on Rural Development, Committee on Agriculture and Forestry, U.S. Senate, 93rd Congress, 2d session, February 27, 1974 (Washington, D.C.: Government Printing Office, 1974), p. 7.

[7] Ibid., p. 8.

[8] Brian Noble, "How to Improve Rural Transportation Systems," *Appalachia* 5, 5 (April 1972): 21–23.

[9] *Proposal for a Transportation System Demonstration Project* (Ridgway, Pa.: North Central Pennsylvania Economic Development District, November 1971), p. 1.

[10] Arthur Salzman et al., *Predicting Rural Public Transportation System Effectiveness* (Greensboro: North Carolina A and T State University, The Transportation Institute, 1974), pp. 16–17.

[11] Burkhardt, p. 4.

[12] This section is based primarily on interviews with and materials supplied by Carol J. Kososki, Office of Manpower Planning and Coordination, Division of Administration, Office of the Governor, State of South Carolina; and on interviews with transportation contractors in various parts of South Carolina.

¹³ Ira Kaye, *Public Transit: An Area of Concern for the Rural South* (Atlanta: Task Force on Southern Rural Development, 1975), p. 23.

¹⁴ Lynn M. Daft, *Implications of Higher Fuel Prices for Rural Development Policy* (Atlanta: Task Force on Southern Rural Development, 1975), p. 10.

¹⁵ Bradley W. Perry, "The Welfare Consequences of Increased Energy Costs" (Unpublished paper, Department of Environmental Sciences, University of Virginia, March, 1974). Cited in Daft, p. 10.

Chapter Nine

Summary and Conclusions

The evidence is overwhelming that on average people living in rural areas of the United States are relatively disadvantaged in terms of access to economic opportunity and that this is especially the case for persons remote from metropolitan centers. Admittedly, the "on average" qualification implies that it would be simplistic to assume that living in a rural area is equivalent to personal misfortune. Many people prefer the amenities of a rural residence even if it entails some economic disadvantage. Moreover, in very recent years there has been an unprecedented shift in migration flows, so that there is net migration to nonmetropolitan areas from metropolitan areas. This movement is consistent with the findings of a number of residential location preference surveys which indicate that a higher proportion of persons wish to live in small towns and rural areas than actually live there. More refined surveys suggest that most people probably want the best of both worlds—that is, a nonmetropolitan residence within at least fairly easy commuting distance of a metropolitan center, though not necessarily a large one.

Even though something of a nonmetropolitan renaissance is taking place, it still has not greatly affected millions of rural people who lack access to economic opportunity. There often is little demand for their labor where they live, but the skills that they offer also frequently reflect neglected human resource development. The public policy measures that have been implemented to help overcome these problems have had only limited success. On the demand side, the growth center policies of federal area development agencies such as the Appalachian Regional Commission and the Economic Development Administration have not been very effective in creating jobs in lagging rural areas. One reason has been that the funds appropriated by Congress have been small in relation to the magnitude of the problems dealt with by these agencies. EDA in particular has also spread its scarce resources rather thinly over a considerable amount of territory; its "growth centers" are typically small towns without any real potential for changing the economic destinies of whole regions. The Appalachian Regional Commission has attempted to concentrate its growth center investments in a relatively few places, but the amounts have not been sufficient in themselves to induce accelerated growth of the places involved. On the other hand, the ARC has been highly innovative in its outreach efforts to improve health and education in Appalachia. Unfortunately, the full long run social benefits of these efforts are difficult to measure, especially when many of the beneficiaries migrate outside the region to places with greater economic opportunity.

Even if a well-funded attempt had been made to implement a growth center strategy in the United States, it probably would not have been successful in inducing long run economic growth in lagging regions. The usual version of the growth center approach to regional development assumes (1) that growth can be induced in urban centers with "significant growth potential," and (2) that "spread effects" emanating from the growth centers will bring greater economic opportunity to hinterland areas. Nearly all of the international evidence to date indicates that even if growth can be induced in one or a few selected centers, the economic linkages with other areas are very diffuse—i.e., there are few important spread effects to the target hinterland areas.

Political problems also arise in the formulation and implementation of growth center strategies. The issue of which place or places should be selected is particularly thorny; it usually is resolved by making a large number of small places "growth centers." Furthermore, in our investigations of manpower and area development planning in Tennessee it was found that the designation of growth centers might well have been a disincentive to the places not selected. Both economic development programs and manpower programs in the state have benefited from cooperation among communities and agencies in a multicounty planning district framework, but this cooperation has been secured because each county feels it is receiving its "fair share" of attention. Nevertheless, it may be useful to have at least a vague growth center plan waiting in the wings, because knowledge that a selective, urban-oriented strategy could be applied to an area might well induce the more rural counties to cooperate—within the more equitable district framework—in simulating some of the advantages of a metropolitan area.

The multicounty districts of Tennessee are part of a larger national effort to develop substate regionalism within the federal system. The various states have used their own methods for delineating substate planning and development districts, and, not unexpectedly, district boundaries often have been based as much on political expediency as on purely economic factors. However, scholars and federal government officials have delineated a number of nationally exhaustive sets of functional economic areas. Most of these are based on the nodal-functional principle—that is, they are relatively self-contained labor market areas having an urban core and (except in megalopolitan areas) a nonmetropolitan hinterland.

In Chapter Four the various theoretically derived regionalizations of the United States were compared with the substate planning and development districts designated by the governors. The best known delineation, and one in terms of which a wide variety of data has been assembled, is that made by the Bureau of Economic Analysis (BEA), U.S. Department of Commerce. For purposes of functional labor market analysis the 173 BEA regions have many advantages, the most important being a clear recognition that the spatial organization of the nation is closely related to its urban system. BEA region delineations also emphasize interdependencies between nonmetropolitan counties and SMSAs and they provide a highly useful vehicle for analyzing the welfare consequences of access to SMSAs. Unfortunately, though, the relevance of the BEA regions to problems of hinterland areas where few, if any, workers commute to a city is very limited, despite the fact that the total population living in such areas is far from negligible.

Thus, in choosing spatial units of analysis for studies primarily concerned with nonmetropolitan labor markets—and especially areas where few workers commute to an SMSA—one would be better advised to use Basic Economic Research Areas. Like the BEA regions, the 482 BERAs are nodal-functional in nature, but their respective urban centers range down in size to 25,000 inhabitants, and some BERAs in sparsely settled territories do not contain a center of even this modest size. The size and location of the BERAs also have at least a rough correspondence with the substate planning and development districts; in many instances where they differ correspondence could be achieved with only slight modification in the BERA delineation criteria. Finally, empirical analyses have shown that BERAs and substate planning and development districts have similar descriptive properties for many key economic variables.

In addition to putting pressure on the states to create multicounty planning units within which federal programs could be coordinated, the Office of Management and Budget, through its Circular A-95 (July 24, 1969), has sought to establish a network of state, regional and metropolitan planning and development clearinghouses. The clearinghouse function is usually lodged in the substate planning and development districts and involves efforts to receive and disseminate information about proposed projects; to coordinate applications for federal assistance; to act as a liaison between federal agencies contemplating federal development projects; and to perform the evaluation of the state, regional or metropolitan significance of federal or federally assisted projects. Progress in these regards depends heavily on the ability of state governors to create economically (as well as politically) meaningful functional planning units and to compel the various agencies to coordinate their activities within this framework. Even more important, if the A–95 review process is to be effective there must be regional plans against which the consistency of projects and programs can be evaluated. At present such plans are largely nonexistent, though efforts are being made to institute them in some states. Commitment to substate planning and the A–95 review process varies widely among the states, but it tends to be strongest in states with relatively large nonmetropolitan populations. In Kentucky, for example, a new integrated grant administration program will allow funding for all major programs carried out by the substate planning districts to be brought together within one application. As pointed out in Chapter Five, this means that for the first time each district's planning, service and technical assistance functions can be designed and implemented as a part of an administratively uniform package, rather than being a product of scores of separate categorical projects. Such an innovation could not be introduced without a climate of partnership between the state and the substate districts.

Unfortunately, there has been a particular lack of integration of manpower programs into substate regional planning. Although many rural districts want to increase the demand for local labor by attracting new firms, few seem equally interested in upgrading the quality of the local labor force. In connection with the present study, rural manpower officials in 31 states were asked whether or not manpower planning was carried out in the context of substate regional planning. The replies indicated that this is rarely the case, and where it is the attempt may not be successful. In the majority of replies the officials communicated attitudes of ignorance, indifference, futility or hostility. Some of these responses may well have been reasonable reactions to the poor quality of substate planning efforts. Yet the evidence is consistent with a major evaluation of federal activities affecting the location of economic development, where it was found that policy officials in the U.S. Department of Labor have only a vague perception of the relationship between manpower programs and economic development strategy. The study points out that "[a]n extensive system of collection and evaluation of labor statistics exists but it is not actively used to suggest regional economic trends or possible development strategies;" and that "[m]anpower programs almost completely omit objectives of mobility and migration; evaluations of programs rarely analyze the impact of training upon mobility. The resulting policies in no way seek to introduce the concept of economic development into program operations."[1]

---

[1] *Federal Activities Affecting Location of Economic Development*, vol. II, pt. I, Appendix A: Program Analysis (Washington, D.C.: Center for Political Research, Research Services Division, November 1970), p. I–26.

These judgments were made prior to the enactment of the Comprehensive Employment and Training Act of 1973. As discussed in Chapter Six, CETA essentially decentralizes and decategorizes manpower programs. Whereas the latter had been operated on a project-by-project basis through separate sponsors, the secretary of labor now makes block grants to some 500 local and state prime sponsors who are supposed to plan and operate manpower programs to meet local needs. In most rural areas, services under CETA are provided by the state, operating as a "balance-of-state" prime sponsor. Under the present system, states and localities determine what mix of programs best serves their needs, though Department of Labor technical assistance is available. Neither CETA nor Department of Labor regulations provide much guidance to local governments in essentially rural areas, though it is clear that local officials in rural areas will have to develop working relations with their state house rather than the Department of Labor. Governors are given wide discretion and it is not surprising that emerging state structures reflect a variety of responses and varying degrees of decentralization. However, as previously noted, there is little indication so far that economic development planning within the substate planning district context and manpower program planning are being effectively integrated. One notable exception is in the state of Tennessee, whose efforts in these regards are discussed in detail in Chapter Six. The Tennessee case deserves careful monitoring because its successes—and problems—should provide valuable insights to other states.

Perhaps the major task of decentralized manpower planning is to give nonmetropolitan workers greater access to economic opportunity. This involves not only developing manpower skills, but also providing better spatial access to jobs. Despite economic conditions that make private automobile ownership difficult and despite the paucity of public transportation in rural areas, rural industries often draw their labor forces from remarkably wide geographic areas. In 1970, 23 percent of rural workers worked outside their county of residence; this was the case for only 18 percent of urban workers. In the same year, rural nonpoor families spent 17.4 percent of their budgets on transportation; the corresponding values for rural poor families and urban families were 10.8 percent and 11.6 percent, respectively (see Table 8-1). The relatively high figure for rural nonpoor workers no doubt reflects the fact that rural residents drive longer distances to work. Some rural poor people may keep their transportation costs down by carpooling, but their relatively low transportation outlays more likely mean that they are unemployed or underemployed in the local labor market.

Those who maintain that commuting can overcome the access problem usually draw their examples from two particular kinds of nonmetropolitan situations. The first consists of areas in proximity to SMSAs; it was shown in Chapter One that economic welfare in nonmetropolitan areas tends to be associated directly with ability to commute to an SMSA. The second consists of areas where a fairly large number of persons live within commuting distance of one another. It has been argued that even in nonmetropolitan areas there are labor markets with upwards of 100,000 inhabitants which, with proper planning, could simulate the advantages of a metropolitan area. In Chapter Seven a set of 49 such nonmetropolitan regions was studied in relation to relatively nearby SMSAs and to dispersed urban regions. The latter are multicounty chains or clusters of medium-size and small cities—e.g., the North Carolina Piedmont.

The 49 nonmetropolitan regions were selected on the basis of the following criteria: (1) the counties involved were beyond normal commuting distance to an SMSA, (2) the people within the region for the most part lived within commuting distance of one another and (3) the counties in the region had a total population of at least 100,000 persons. State rural manpower officials were contacted to verify the accuracy of the delineation of the nonmetropolitan regions.

Within the areas studied, workers in the nonmetropolitan regions do not use public transportation to get to work to the same extent as workers in SMSAs or dispersed urban regions. Only 1.44 percent of nonmetropolitan workers use public transportation, compared with 5.92 percent in SMSAs and 3.30 percent in dispersed urban areas.

As might be expected, SMSAs outside the South have higher median income levels than any other type of area studied. For areas outside the South, nonmetropolitan regions have median family incomes significantly below those in SMSAs and dispersed urban regions. Yet they are significantly above those in the nonmetropolitan regions of the South, and not significantly different from Southern SMSAs and Southern dispersed urban regions. Within the South, SMSA and dispersed urban region median incomes are not significantly different, but both have significantly higher levels than nonmetropolitan regions. Geographic differences in incidence of poverty follow similar patterns.

If the relevant data were not disaggregated regionally it would appear that the proportion of workers using public transportation to work is directly related to median family income and inversely related to poverty incidence. Disaggregation reveals a different picture. For example, Southern nonmetropolitan workers use public transportation to a significantly greater extent than their counterparts outside the South, yet they are in a significantly worse position with respect to median family income and incidence of poverty. Moreover, the proportion of the labor force that commutes to work is greater in the nonmetropolitan South than in other nonmetropolitan areas.

Measures of commuting outside of region of residence indicate that long distance commuting is significantly greater in nonmetropolitan regions than in either SMSAs or dispersed urban regions. The results of regression analyses suggest that the kinds of nonmetropolitan regions considered in Chapter Seven are relatively self-contained for professional and managerial categories of residents, but not for black or older workers. Blacks appear to have difficulty commuting and the few who do often have to go to work places outside their region of residence. The proportion of commuters who commute from nonmetropolitan regions to work is significantly and directly related to median age.

Despite the obvious willingness of many rural residents to commute to work, lack of transportation clearly limits access to employment opportunities for many disadvantaged persons. This problem no doubt will be made more acute by the energy crisis. In the kinds of nonmetropolitan regions examined in Chapter Seven—that is, regions with at least 100,000 inhabitants within commuting distance of one another—it should be possible to organize transportation systems to link underemployed and unemployed persons with job opportunities more effectively. In the late 1960s the Office of Economic Opportunity provided demonstration grants for rural transportation prototype systems. By 1972, about 50 such projects were being operated under the auspices of local community action agencies, which had consistently identified transportation as a major problem area. Because of cutbacks in OEO funding most of these projects have either disappeared or else been severely curtailed. However, even with subsidies it was evident that there were few people among the target populations who were willing and able to pay for transportation. Although the Federal Highway Act of 1973 authorized a program of rural public highway demonstration projects, funds have not been appropriated at this writing.

Perhaps the most innovative recent rural transportation program is that being instituted in South Carolina with Comprehensive Employment and Training Act funds. This program, which was discussed in detail in the previous chapter, is especially interesting because of its manpower orientation. The OEO projects typically involved the transportation of poor and elderly persons seeking shopping, medical and social service facilities. The South Carolina program is addressed to the transportation needs of manpower program enrollees, though one of its best features is that it is sufficiently flexible to serve more comprehensive needs. It is a cooperative effort between the state's office of manpower planning and coordination and 11 transportation contractors (mostly community action agencies) in the respective substate planning districts. An unusual feature of the program is that contractors are reimbursed for manpower enrollee transportation on a passenger mile basis, rather than on the vehicle mile basis favored by other state agencies. The rationale for this approach is that it gives an incentive to contractors to do their best in providing efficient, effective routing and scheduling, thereby eliminating deadheading as much as possible. Also, once manpower enrollees are served, contractors can obtain additional revenues by selling excess capacity to other state agencies and organizations serving the transportation needs of disadvantaged rural residents.

Although transportation is an essential element in giving rural residents better access to services and employment opportunities, it is only one element in the constellation of change that must take place if the relative disadvantages of nonmetropolitan areas are to be reduced—if not entirely overcome—in the foreseeable future. Rural counties must learn to combine their forces within a substate planning district framework so that they can more effectively simulate the manpower and other services that are better developed in metropolitan labor markets. Innovative approaches will be required to increase access to opportunities through improved communications and information systems, more know-how in obtaining federal grants or in the efficient use of revenue-sharing funds and the sharing of complementary public facilities. A major drawback in this regard is the lack of capable personnel to prepare operationally feasible plans. Thus, if innovation diffusion processes are to benefit nonmetropolitan areas—and especially the more lagging regions—or at least benefit them earlier than at present, some new forms of quasi-public entrepreneurship appear to be indicated. The necessary vehicle may be a nonprofit local development corporation willing to pay the price needed to attract talented leadership to relatively remote places.

In any event, development of relatively lagging regions requires increased linkages with more dynamic regions and sectors of the national economy. The issue is fundamentally one of increasing opportunities to benefit from the external economies found in more urbanized areas. Moreover, the notion of increasing access should be understood in the broadest sense, implying openness to the whole range of processes of innovation diffusion and institution-building in such areas as health, education, services, increased communication and leadership development. In the absence of increased access, efforts to attract new industry may at best simply result in increases in the scale of economic activity, without basically altering the combination or mix of basic factors of production. Economic development—as contrasted with growth of scale—involves changing ways of doing things: creating products and services, inventing new techniques, discovering new resources, gaining access to markets, innovating organizational arrangements and changing the mix of inputs. If past history is the only guide to lagging regions, expansion of traditional economic activity will result in growth of regional product, but it may also retard genuine development by inhibiting innovation diffusion and creative institution building.

Appendixes

Appendix A
Nonmetropolitan Regions

State	Principal City	Population 1970	Counties	Population 1970	Region Code	Comparison SMSA
Alabama	Florence	34,031	Lauderdale Colbert	68,111 49,632 117,743	1701	Huntsville
Alabama	Auburn	22,767	Lee Macon Chambers	61,268 24,841 36,356 122,465	1702	Montgomery
Alabama	Dothan	36,733	Houston Dale Coffee	56,574 52,938 34,872 144,384	1703	Pensacola
Arkansas	Hot Springs	35,631	Garland Hot Spring Clark	54,131 21,963 21,537 97,631	1706	Little Rock
Arkansas	El Dorado	25,283	Union Ouachita Columbia	45,428 30,896 25,952 102,276	1707	Fort Smith
California	Chico	19,580	Butte Yuba Sutter	101,969 44,736 41,935 188,640	1109	Sacramento
California	San Luis Obispo	28,036	San Luis Obispo	105,690 105,690	1110	Santa Barbara

Appendix A continued

State	Principal City	Population 1970	Counties	Population 1970	Region Code	Comparison SMSA
Georgia	Valdosta	32,303	Lowndes	55,112	1749	Columbus
			Lanier	5,031		
			Irwin	8,036		
			Cook	12,129		
			Echols	1,924		
			Brooks	13,743		
			Berrien	11,556		
				107,531		
Idaho	Twin Falls	21,914	Twin Falls	41,807	1611	Boise City
			Gooding	8,645		
			Jerome	10,253		
			Minidoka	15,731		
			Cassia	17,017		
			Lincoln	3,057		
			Blaine	5,749		
				102,259		
Illinois	Dixon	18,147	Lee	37,947	1212	Rockford
			Whiteside	62,877		
				100,824		
Illinois	Marion	11,724	Williamson	49,021	1247	Terre Haute
			Franklin	38,329		
			Saline	25,721		
				113,071		
Indiana	Marion	39,607	Grant	83,955	1213	South Bend
			Wabash	35,553		
			Huntington	34,970		
				154,478		

State	City		Counties			
Indiana	Kokomo	44,042	Howard Cass Miami	83,198 40,456 39,246 162,900	1214	South Bend
Iowa	Burlington	32,366	Des Moines Lee Henry	46,982 42,996 18,114 108,092	1515	Davenport- Rock Island- Moline
Kansas	Hutchinson	36,885	Reno McPherson Harvey	60,765 24,778 27,236 112,779	1516	Wichita
Kentucky	Paducah	31,627	McCracken Graves Marshall	58,281 30,939 20,381 109,601	1717	Evansville
Louisiana	Houma	30,922	Terrebonne St. Mary Lafourche	76,049 60,752 68,941 205,742	1708	New Orleans
Maine	Augusta	21,945	Kennebec Somerset	95,247 40,597 135,844	1425	Portland
Maryland	Hagerstown	35,862	Washington Frederick Berkeley, WV Franklin, PA	103,829 84,927 36,356 100,833 325,945	1326	York
Minnesota	Mankato	30,895	Blue Earth Nicollet Brown	52,322 24,518 28,887 105,727	1527	Sioux City

Appendix A continued

State	Principal City	Population 1970	Counties	Population 1970	Region Code	Comparison SMSA
Minnesota	St. Cloud	39,691	Benton	20,841	1528	Minneapolis-St. Paul
			Sherburne	18,344		
			Stearns	95,400		
			Morrison	26,949		
				161,534		
Minnesota	Austin	25,074	Mower	43,783	1529	Rochester
			Rice	41,582		
			Steele	26,931		
			Freeborn	38,064		
				150,360		
Mississippi	Tupelo	20,471	Lee	46,148	1704	Memphis
			Alcorn	27,179		
			Prentiss	20,133		
			Union	19,096		
				112,556		
Mississippi	Greenville	39,648	Washington	70,581	1705	Jackson
			Leflore	42,111		
			Bolivar	49,409		
			Sunflower	37,047		
				199,148		
Missouri	Sedalia	22,847	Pettis	34,137	1520	Kansas City
			Saline	24,837		
			Cooper	14,732		
			Johnson	34,172		
				107,878		
Montana	Butte	23,368	Silver Bow	41,981	1621	Great Falls
			Lewis and Clark	33,281		
			Powell	6,660		

State	City	City Pop.	County	County Pop.	Total	Code	MSA
			Deer Lodge	15,652			
			Jefferson	5,238	102,812		
Nebraska	Grand Island	31,269	Hall	42,851		1522	Omaha
			Adams	30,553			
			Buffalo	31,222	104,626		
New York	Ogdensburg	14,554	St. Lawrence	111,991	111,991	1323	Utica-Rome
North Carolina	Kinston	23,020	Lenoir	55,204		1739	Wilmington
			Pamlico	9,467			
			Craven	62,554			
			Onslow	103,126			
			Jones	9,779	240,130		
North Carolina	Hickory	20,569	Burke	60,364		1724	Asheville
			Catawba	90,873			
			Caldwell	56,699			
			Alexander	19,466	227,402		
Ohio	Sidney	16,332	Shelby	37,748		1233	Dayton
			Logan	35,072			
			Champaign	30,491	103,311		
Ohio	Zanesville	33,045	Muskingum	77,826		1244	Champaign-Urbana
			Coshocton	33,486			
			Guernsey	37,665	148,977		
Ohio	Chillicothe	24,842	Ross	61,211		1245	Columbus
			Fayette	25,461			
			Highland	28,996	115,668		

Appendix A continued

State	Principal City	Population 1970	Counties	Population 1970	Region Code	Comparison SMSA
Ohio	Sandusky	32,674	Erie Huron Sandusky	75,909 49,587 60,983 186,479	1246	Toledo
Oklahoma	Muskogee	37,331	Muskogee Okmulgee McIntosh Pittsburg	59,542 35,358 12,472 37,521 144,893	1834	Tulsa
Oregon	Medford	28,454	Jackson Josephine	94,533 35,746 130,279	1135	Eugene
Pennsylvania	Meadville	16,573	Crawford Venango	81,342 62,353 143,695	1336	Erie
South Carolina	Florence	25,997	Florence Sumter Darlington Lee	89,636 79,425 53,442 18,323 240,826	1740	Columbia
South Carolina	Anderson	27,556	Anderson Laurens Greenwood Abbeville	105,474 49,713 49,686 21,112 225,985	1741	Greenville
South Dakota	Rapid City	43,836	Pennington Lawrence	59,349 17,453	1542	Fargo- Moorhead

State	City		Counties			
South Dakota	Aberdeen	26,476	Fall River	7,505	1543	Fargo-Moorhead
			Meade	16,618		
			Custer	4,698		
				105,623		
			Brown	36,920		
			Codington	19,140		
			Beadle	20,877		
			Spink	10,595		
			Day	8,713		
			Clark	5,515		
				101,760		
Tennessee	Jackson	39,996	Madison	65,774	1718	Memphis
			Gibson	47,871		
				113,645		
Tennessee	Bristol, Tennessee-Virginia	34,921	Sullivan	127,329	1719	Knoxville
			Washington	73,924		
			Hawkins	33,757		
			Carter	43,259		
				278,269		
Tennessee	Cookeville	14,270	Putnam	35,487	1748	Nashville
			Cumberland	20,773		
			Jackson	8,141		
			Overton	14,866		
			Smith	12,509		
			White	16,355		
				108,131		
Texas	Paris	23,441	Lamar	36,062	1737	Texarkana
			Hunt	47,948		
			Hopkins	20,710		
			Delta	4,927		
				109,647		

Appendix A continued

State	Principal City	Population 1970	Counties	Population 1970	Region Code	Comparison SMSA
Texas	Lufkin	23,049	Angelina	49,349	1738	Tyler
			Nacogdoches	36,362		
			Cherokee	32,008		
				117,719		
Virginia	Staunton	24,504	Independent city	24,504	1730	Lynchburg
			Augusta	44,220		
			Rockingham	47,890		
			Independent cities of Waynesboro and Harrisonbury	31,312		
				147,926		
West Virginia	Beckley	19,884	Raleigh	70,080	1731	Charleston
			Wyoming	30,095		
			Fayette	49,332		
			Summers	13,213		
				162,720		
Wisconsin	Wausau	32,806	Marathon	97,457	1232	Appleton-Oshkosh; Green Bay
			Lincoln	23,499		
			Langlade	19,220		
			Portage	47,541		
			Wood	65,362		
				253,079		

Appendix B

Comparison SMSAs

SMSA	Population, 1970	County Components	Area Code
Appleton-Oshkosh; Green Bay, Wisconsin	435,192	Outagamie Winnebago Calumet Brown	2232
Asheville, North Carolina	145,056	Buncombe	2724
Atlanta, Georgia	1,390,247	Clayton Cobb DeKalb Fulton Gwinnett	2749
Boise City, Idaho	112,230	Ada	2611
Champaign-Urbana, Illinois	163,281	Champaign	2244
Charleston, West Virginia	229,515	Kanawha	2731
Columbia, South Carolina	322,880	Lexington Richland	2740
Columbus, Georgia	238,584	Muscogee Chattahoochee Russell, Alabama	2750
Columbus, Ohio	916,228	Delaware Franklin Pickaway	2245
Davenport-Rock Island-Moline, Iowa	362,638	Scott Rock Island, Illinois Henry, Illinois	2215
Dayton, Ohio	852,531	Miami Greene Montgomery Preble	2233
Erie, Pennsylvania	263,654	Erie	2336
Eugene, Oregon	215,401	Lane	2135
Evansville, Indiana	232,775	Vanderburgh Warrick Henderson, Kentucky	2217

Appendix B continued

SMSA	Population, 1970	County Components	Area Code
Fargo-Moorhead, North Dakota	120,261	Cass Clay, Minnesota	2542
Fort Smith, Arkansas	160,421	Crawford Sebastian Sequoyah, Oklahoma LeFlore, Oklahoma	2707
Great Falls, Montana	81,804	Cascade	2621
Greenville, South Carolina	299,730	Greenville Pickens	2741
Huntsville, Alabama	228,239	Limestone Madison	2701
Jackson, Mississippi	258,906	Hinds Rankin	2705
Kansas City, Missouri	1,256,327	Cass Jackson Clay Platte Wyandotte, Kansas Johnson, Kansas	2520
Knoxville, Tennessee	400,337	Anderson Blount Knox	2719
Little Rock–North Little Rock, Arkansas	323,296	Saline Pulaski	2706
Lynchburg, Virginia	123,474	Amherst Campbell Independent city of Lynchburg	2730
Memphis, Tennessee	770,217	Shelby Crittenden, Arkansas	2704
Minneapolis-St. Paul, Minnesota	1,813,587	Anoka Dakota Hennepin Ramsey Washington	2528
Montgomery, Alabama	201,451	Elmore Montgomery	2702
Nashville, Tennessee	541,142	Sumner Davidson Wilson	2748
New Orleans, Louisiana	1,046,470	Jefferson St. Bernard St. Tammany Orleans	2708
Omaha, Nebraska	542,646	Pottawattamie, Iowa Douglas, Nebraska Sarpy, Nebraska	2522

Appendix B continued

SMSA	Population, 1970	County Components	Area Code
Pensacola, Florida	243,075	Santa Rosa Escambia	2703
Portland, Maine	141,625	Cumberland	2425
Rochester, Minnesota	84,104	Olmsted	2529
Rockford, Illinois	272,063	Winnebago Boone	2212
Sacramento, California	803,610	Placer Sacramento Yolo	2109
Santa Barbara, California	264,324	Santa Barbara	2110
Sioux City, Iowa	116,189	Woodbury Dakota, Nebraska	2527
South Bend, Indiana	280,031	St. Joseph Marshall	2213
Terre Haute, Indiana	175,143	Clay Sullivan Vermillion Vigo	2247
Texarkana, Texas	101,198	Bowie Miller, Arkansas	2737
Toledo, Ohio	692,488	Wood Lucas Monroe, Michigan	2246
Tulsa, Oklahoma	475,264	Creek Osage Tulsa	2834
Tyler, Texas	97,096	Smith	2738
Utica-Rome, New York	340,670	Oneida Herkimer	2323
Wichita, Kansas	389,352	Sedgwick Butler	2516
Wilmington, North Carolina	107,219	Brunswick New Hanover	2739
York, Pennsylvania	329,540	Adams York	2326

Appendix C

Dispersed Urban Regions

Region Name	Counties	Population, 1970	Region Code
Albuquerque-Espanola, New Mexico	Bernalillo, New Mexico	315,774	3801
	Santa Fe, New Mexico	53,756	
	Los Alamos, New Mexico	15,198	
	Sandoval, New Mexico	3,714	
		388,442	
Biloxi-Gulfport, Mississippi; Mobile, Alabama; Pensacola, Florida	Harrison, Mississippi	134,582	3702
	Jackson, Mississippi	87,975	
	Mobile, Alabama	317,308	
	Escambia, Florida	205,334	
	Santa Rosa, Florida	37,741	
	Baldwin, Alabama	59,382	
		842,322	
Champaign-Urbana-Peoria, Illinois	Champaign, Illinois	163,281	3203
	McLean, Illinois	104,389	
	Peoria, Illinois	195,318	
	Tazewell, Illinois	118,649	
	Woodford, Illinois	28,012	
		609,649	
Waterloo, Iowa; Davenport-Rock Island-Moline, Iowa-Illinois	Black Hawk, Iowa	132,916	3504
	Linn, Iowa	163,213	
	Johnson, Iowa	72,127	
	Scott, Iowa	142,687	
	Rock Island, Illinois	166,734	
	Henry, Illinois	53,217	
	Cedar, Iowa	17,655	
	Benton, Iowa	22,885	
	Buchanan, Iowa	21,762	
		793,196	
Saginaw-Bay City-Midland, Michigan	Saginaw, Michigan	219,743	3205
	Bay City, Michigan	117,339	
	Midland, Michigan	63,769	
		400,851	

Appendix C continued

Region Name	Counties	Population, 1970	Region Code
Augusta-Savannah, Georgia; Columbia-Charleston, South Carolina	Richmond, Georgia	162,437	3706
	Aiken, South Carolina	91,023	
	Richland, South Carolina	233,868	
	Charleston, South Carolina	247,650	
	Chatham, Georgia	187,816	
	Orangeburg, South Carolina	69,789	
	Lexington, South Carolina	89,012	
	Calhoun, South Carolina	10,780	
	Dorchester, South Carolina	32,276	
	Berkeley, South Carolina	56,199	
	Colleton, South Carolina	27,622	
	Beaufort, South Carolina	51,136	
	Jasper, South Carolina	11,885	
	Barnwell, South Carolina	17,176	
	Bamberg, South Carolina	51,199	
	Allendale, South Carolina	9,783	
	Hampton, South Carolina	15,878	
		1,365,529	
Greenville, South Carolina; Greenville, North Carolina	Pickens, South Carolina	58,956	3707
	Greenville, South Carolina	240,774	
	Spartanburg, South Carolina	173,724	
	Cherokee, South Carolina	36,791	
	York, South Carolina	85,216	
	Gaston, North Carolina	148,415	
	Mecklenburg, North Carolina	354,656	
	Union, North Carolina	54,714	
	Cabarrus, North Carolina	74,629	
	Rowan, North Carolina	90,035	
	Iredell, North Carolina	72,197	
	Davidson, North Carolina	95,627	
	Forsyth, North Carolina	214,348	
	Yadkin, North Carolina	24,599	
	Randolph, North Carolina	76,358	
	Guilford, North Carolina	288,645	
	Alamance, North Carolina	96,362	
	Durham, North Carolina	132,681	
	Orange, North Carolina	57,707	
	Wake, North Carolina	229,006	
	Edgecombe, North Carolina	52,341	
	Nash, North Carolina	59,122	
	Wilson, North Carolina	57,486	
	Pitt, North Carolina	73,900	
	Davie, North Carolina	18,855	
		2,867,144	
Fort Wayne, Indiana; Lima, Ohio	Allen, Indiana	280,455	3208
	Allen, Ohio	111,144	
	Putnam, Ohio	31,134	
	Van Wert, Ohio	29,194	
		451,927	

Appendix C continued

Region Name	Counties	Population, 1970	Region Code
Salem-Corvallis-Eugene, Oregon	Marion, Oregon	151,309	3109
	Polk, Oregon	35,349	
	Benton, Oregon	53,776	
	Linn, Oregon	71,914	
	Lane, Oregon	215,401	
		527,749	
Austin-Temple-Waco, Texas	Travis, Texas	295,516	3810
	Williamson, Texas	37,305	
	Bell, Texas	124,483	
	McLennan, Texas	147,553	
		604,857	
McAllen-Pharr-Edinburg-Brownsville-Harlingen-San Benito, Texas	Hidalgo, Texas	181,535	0011
	Cameron, Texas	140,368	
	Willacy, Texas	15,570	
		337,473	
Tyler-Longview-Marshall, Texas; Shreveport, Louisiana	Smith, Texas	97,096	3712
	Rusk, Texas	34,102	
	Gregg, Texas	75,929	
	Harrison, Texas	44,841	
	Bossier, Louisiana	63,703	
	Caddo, Louisiana	230,184	
		545,855	
Beaumont-Port Arthur-Orange, Texas; Lake Charles, Louisiana	Jefferson, Texas	244,773	3713
	Orange, Texas	71,170	
	Calcasieu, Louisiana	145,415	
		461,358	
Roanoke-Lynchburg-Danville, Virginia	Roanoke, Virginia	67,339	3714
	Amherst, Virginia	26,072	
	Campbell, Virginia	43,319	
	Pittsylvania, Virginia	58,789	
	Henry, Virginia	50,901	
	Bedford, Virginia	26,728	
	Franklin, Virginia	28,163	
	Independent cities of		
	Roanoke	92,115	
	Salem	21,982	
	Lynchburg	54,083	
	Danville	46,391	
	Martinsville	19,653	
	Bedford, Virginia	6,011	
		541,546	
Charleston, West Virginia; Huntington-Ashland, West Virginia-Kentucky	Kanawha, West Virginia	229,515	3715
	Cabell, West Virginia	106,918	
	Wayne, West Virginia	37,581	
	Boyd, Kentucky	52,376	
	Lawrence, Ohio	56,868	
	Putnam, West Virginia	27,625	
		510,883	

Appendix C continued

Region Name	Counties	Population, 1970	Region Code
Appleton-Oshkosh-Green Bay, Wisconsin	Winnebago, Wisconsin	129,931	3216
	Calumet, Wisconsin	27,604	
	Outagamie, Wisconsin	119,356	
	Brown, Wisconsin	158,244	
		435,135	
Madison, Wisconsin; Rockford, Illinois	Dane, Wisconsin	290,272	3217
	Rock, Wisconsin	131,970	
	Winnebago, Illinois	246,623	
	Boone, Illinois	25,440	
		694,305	
Bakersfield-Fresno, California	Kern, California	329,162	3118
	Tulare, California	188,322	
	Fresno, California	413,053	
	Kings, California	66,019	
		996,556	
Harrisburg-York-Lancaster-Reading, Pennsylvania	York, Pennsylvania	272,603	3319
	Adams, Pennsylvania	56,937	
	Lancaster, Pennsylvania	320,079	
	Berks, Pennsylvania	296,382	
	Dauphin, Pennsylvania	223,834	
	Cumberland, Pennsylvania	158,177	
	Perry, Pennsylvania	28,615	
	Lebanon, Pennsylvania	99,665	
		1,456,292	
Wilkes-Barre–Hazelton–Scranton, Pennsylvania; Binghamton, New York	Luzerne, Pennsylvania	342,301	3320
	Lackawanna, Pennsylvania	234,107	
	Susquehanna, Pennsylvania	34,344	
	Broome, New York	221,815	
	Tioga, New York	46,513	
		879,080	

INDEX

About the Author

Niles M. Hansen is Professor of Economics and Director, Center for Economic Development, at the University of Texas. From 1975 to 1977 he is also Project Leader, Urban and Regional Systems, International Institute for Applied Systems Analysis, Laxenburg, Austria.

He is the author of *French Regional Planning; France in the Modern World; Rural Poverty and the Urban Crisis; Intermediate-Size Cities as Growth Centers; Location Preferences, Migration and Regional Growth; The Future of Nonmetropolitan America; The Challenge of Urban Growth;* and the editor of *Growth Centers in Regional Economic Development and Public Policy;* and *Regional Economic Development: The Experience of Nine Western Countries.* He also has contributed numerous articles to professional journals in economics and social sciences.